At Issue

| Rebuilding the
| World Trade Center Site

Other Books in the At Issue Series:

At Issue

Rebuilding the World Trade Center Site

Margaret Haerens, Book Editor

GREENHAVEN PRESS
A part of Gale, Cengage Learning

Detroit • New York • San Francisco • New Haven, Conn • Waterville, Maine • London

Elizabeth Des Chenes, *Managing Editor*

© 2012 Greenhaven Press, a part of Gale, Cengage Learning.

Gale and Greenhaven Press are registered trademarks used herein under license.

For more information, contact:
Greenhaven Press
27500 Drake Rd.
Farmington Hills, MI 48331-3535
Or you can visit our Internet site at gale.cengage.com

For product information and technology assistance, contact us at

Gale Customer Support, 1-800-877-4253
For permission to use material from this text or product, submit all requests online at
www.cengage.com/permissions

Further permissions questions can be emailed to permissionrequest@cengage.com

Articles in Greenhaven Press anthologies are often edited for length to meet page requirements. In addition, original titles of these works are changed to clearly present the main thesis and to explicitly indicate the author's opinion. Every effort is made to ensure that Greenhaven Press accurately reflects the original intent of the authors. Every effort has been made to trace the owners of copyrighted material.

Cover Image copyright © Images.com/Corbis.

LIBRARY OF CONGRESS CATALOGING-IN-PUBLICATION DATA

Rebuilding the World Trade Center / Margaret Haerens, book editor.
      p. cm. -- (At issue)
   Includes bibliographical references and index.
      ISBN 978-0-7377-5592-3 (hardcover : alk. paper) -- ISBN 978-0-7377-5593-0
(pbk. : alk. paper)
   1. World Trade Center Site (New York, N.Y.)--Planning. 2. Urban renewal--New
York (State)--New York. I. Haerens, Margaret. II. Title. III. Series.
   HT177.N5R42 2012
   307.3'216097471--dc23
                                                                    2011029278

Printed in the United States of America
1 2 3 4 5 6 7 15 14 13 12 11

Contents

Introduction

On September 11, 2001, nineteen hijackers took control of four commercial airliners and aimed the planes at targets in the United States. The first plane, American Airlines Flight 11, which took off that morning from Logan International Airport in Boston, hit the North Tower (also known as 1 World Trade Center) of the World Trade Center in New York City at 8:46 AM. United Airlines Flight 175, which also originated at Logan, slammed into the South Tower (also known as 2 World Trade Center) at 9:03 AM. The third airliner crashed into the Pentagon in Arlington, Virginia, just outside Washington, DC. The fourth airliner was diverted from its target (thought to be the White House or US Capitol) and crashed into a field in rural Shanksville, Pennsylvania, after passengers realized what was happening and tried to take back the plane from the hijackers.

Both the North and South Towers of the World Trade Center collapsed within hours of the initial attack, destroying several nearby buildings: 4 World Trade Center, a nine-story office building, was damaged beyond repair and was eventually demolished; 5 World Trade Center, another nine-story office building, was partially damaged by the collapse of the North Tower and was later demolished; 6 World Trade Center was an eight-story building destroyed by falling debris from the North Tower; and 7 World Trade Center was a forty-seven-floor building that caught fire from falling debris during the attacks and collapsed later that day. Also destroyed were the Marriott World Trade Center Hotel, the World Financial Center complex, and St. Nicholas Greek Orthodox Church, all of which were adjacent to the site.

Debate about how to rebuild the World Trade Center complex began almost immediately. Proposals began to pour in, and a joint city-state corporation, the Lower Manhattan Development Corporation (LMDC), was established in July 2002 by Governor George Pataki and then New York City mayor Rudolph Giuliani to oversee and coordinate the rebuilding process.

In 2003, the LMDC launched a design competition to redevelop the site, known as Ground Zero, soliciting plans from architects and planners. The LMDC coordinated with the Port Authority of New York and New Jersey, which owned the site, and Larry Silverstein, who leased the World Trade Center. Feedback from victims' families, residents of the neighborhood, subsequent New York City mayor Michael Bloomberg, and other stakeholders was integral to planning the redevelopment. Many people wanted the site to be designed as a memorial where visitors could pray and remember those who had perished that day. Others insisted that the towers had to be rebuilt as a symbolic rebuke to the terrorists and terrorism. In the end, it was agreed that the complex would be rebuilt but with a magnificent memorial and museum that would inform and remind visitors about what had happened on September 11.

When the first round of designs was rejected, a second competition led to the choice of architect Daniel Libeskind's master plan for a new World Trade Center complex, which centered around a design for the 1,776-foot Freedom Tower. However, conflict between Libeskind and developer Larry Silverstein led to many revisions of the original design. With such symbolic and large-scale projects, it was a long and contentious process to come up with a final design that honored Libeskind's artistic vision and incorporated practical concerns such as added security measures. As Libeskind described the process in an interview for *Fast Company*, "There are always struggles to build a piece of a city. In architecture, you need to build consensus with all the stakeholders. With the Ground Zero project, that meant the families of victims, politicians, investors, and the developer's architect. In the end, I convinced everyone that Ground Zero is not just for the office leaseholders; it's for all of New York." On June 28, 2005, the final design for the Freedom Tower, now known as One World Trade Center, was presented.

The LMDC also launched a competition to design a memorial at the World Trade Center site to commemorate the lives lost on September 11. In January 2004, it was announced that a design by Michael Arad and Peter Walker called "Reflecting Absence" was chosen. In the design, two square pools of water stand in the exact location where the North and South Towers once stood, and are surrounded by a forest of trees to inspire reflection and commemoration.

Once the planning stage of the rebuilding was complete, the construction began. First to be completed was a temporary PATH station (Port Authority Trans-Hudson, a rapid transit railroad) in 2003, which reestablished train service between stops in New Jersey and the World Trade Center subway stop. A permanent station designed by Santiago Calatrava has yet to be completed. In 2006, the rebuilt Seven World Trade Center was officially opened.

In March 2006, construction finally began on the National September 11 Memorial and Museum. A month later, city officials broke ground on the Freedom Tower after months of wrangling and controversy. Yet it seemed like little progress was being made on the key elements of the World Trade Center complex. For years, all that observers could see when they looked over the site was debris and construction equipment. Frustration mounted over the constant construction traffic and noise coupled with the lack of visible-from-street-level rebuilding, and commentators began to question why the process was taking so long. Political infighting and sluggish bureaucratic processes mired the project in delays and sparked more frustration.

By early 2011, however, great progress was being made on the World Trade Center complex. The building of new World

Trade Center Towers Two, Three, Four, and Five was under way and projected to be complete in 2013–2014. The memorial plaza was projected to open on September 11, 2011, ten years after the terrorist attacks. The museum is scheduled to open in 2013. One World Trade Center, once known as the Freedom Tower, is predicted to be completed in 2013, and the permanent transportation hub, which will house the subway and PATH stations, should be finished in 2014.

For most Americans, rebuilding the World Trade Center is essential to the city's recovery and a symbolic victory in the fight against terrorism. As Mayor Bloomberg stated on May 2, 2011, after the death of terrorist mastermind Osama bin Laden, "In the dark days that followed September 11th, we made a solemn commitment that we would rebuild the World Trade Center site. As you can see, Seven World Trade Center is standing and open for business. Four World Trade Center has risen above 25 stories, One World Trade Center is now above 60 stories, and both are stretching higher every day. This is the largest, most complicated construction site in North America—and one of the most important in American history. . . . The construction you see here is a rebuke to all of those who seek to destroy our freedoms and liberties. Nothing will ever return our loved ones—but we are rebuilding from the ashes and the tears a monument to the American spirit. New York's way is ever forward, ever skyward."

At Issue: Rebuilding the World Trade Center Site examines issues surrounding the reconstruction of the site, including controversies over the project's leadership, the lack of progress, and a proposed mosque. It provides insight into the challenges faced by city officials, developers, architects, families, and Americans concerned with rebuilding and commemorating the site of the most devastating attack on American soil.

1

Rebuilding the World Trade Center Is a Complicated Process

Christopher Bonanos

Christopher Bonanos is an author and a senior editor at New York *magazine.*

It is a very complicated process to construct a major building in downtown Manhattan—particularly one as contentious and symbolic as the buildings on the World Trade Center site. Concerns over safety and the efforts to make the building withstand a terrorist attack has tacked on extra time to the project, which, despite the delays, is progressing at an impressive pace. The extra security measures required for this project are a harbinger of New York City's future, as terrorism remains a top concern for city officials.

Nine years into the rebuilding of ground zero, and we're just now getting unstuck. The stakeholders are wrapping up their arguments over who controls which slices of the site, having finally settled on a schematic plan, memorial design, timetable, and financing arrangement that everyone can more or less live with. The public spent a decade being worn down by politics and arguments: [developer] Larry Silverstein versus the Port Authority [of New York and New Jersey]. [New York governor George] Pataki versus the NYPD [New York Police Department]. [Architect Daniel] Libeskind versus [architect]

David Childs. [New York City mayor Michael] Bloomberg versus [New York governor David] Paterson. Memorial designer Michael Arad versus the victims' families. All around those debates swirled the question of whether, economically, this project makes any sense at all, dumping as it does 12 million square feet of office space onto a now-deflated commercial market. Even if you did believe the whole thing should happen, it has been excruciating to watch the site get caught in the old New York snarl of permit agencies and sluggish bureaucracies and every possible variety of red tape.

The Most Difficult Construction Site

Those issues, at least, are not physical realities; they're obstacles based on human nature. Yet, for a long time, they obscured the perhaps even greater problem of building on what is probably the most difficult construction site in history. The architects and engineers involved have known this all along, of course, and now that construction is roaring forward, the rest of us can see what they've been up against. Every bit of land at ground zero is crowded with supplies, workers, and rising steel and concrete. One World Trade Center (the skyscraper formerly known as the Freedom Tower) is 26 stories high and beginning to poke its head into the downtown skyline. Even at quarter-height, its density and bulk are evident, and you can start to grasp how jammed up against the PATH [rapid transit railroad] tracks it is. Its neighbor at Four World Trade is up to about five floors, hard by the 1 train [subway] that continually rattles through the center of the site. The two memorial pools are framed out, and underground construction is moving forward on [architect/engineer] Santiago Calatrava's swoopy transportation hub. Foundation work for Towers 2 and 3 starts next month [June 2010], and the contaminated Deutsche Bank building, looming over the southern end of the site, will come down later this year to make way for Tower 5.

Libeskind's abiding idea—five towers standing guard around a sunken memorial—is inching toward reality.

Actually, "five towers" is a misnomer. It's really all one giant sixteen-acre mega-building, with many zones held by many stakeholders, their structures intermingled "like metastasized synapses in the brain," says T.J. Gottesdiener, the partner at Skidmore, Owings & Merrill [SOM] who's going to end up spending at least a decade of his life directing his [architecture] firm's chunk of the job. The buildings' foundations and underpinnings are seven levels deep, all knitted together, and in the future, as you walk around the concourse levels, you will constantly be changing jurisdictions, sometimes every few feet: in Port Authority territory here, on MTA [Metropolitan Transportation Authority] turf there, entering privately developed space around the corner.

What people don't realize is, setting the foundations, doing the preliminary work below grade before the tower could even be visible to the public, was three years in the making.

That's a major reason the construction has appeared even slower than it has been: A lot of significant work has taken place out of sight. One World Trade alone has 350,000 square feet of space beneath the surface. (For comparison, that's the entire size of its 25-story neighbor at 44 Wall Street.) Chris Ward, executive director of the Port Authority, puts it this way: "What people don't realize is, setting the foundations, doing the preliminary work below grade before the tower could even be visible to the public, was three years in the making."

Two tunnels run through the sixteen-acre World Trade Center site: the 1 subway line, north to south, and the PATH tubes, looping through and going directly under One World Trade. This is not an abnormal obstacle on its own; New York architects and engineers deal with subway tunnels under their buildings all the time. Consider, though, what they have to do here, since the underground memorial is bisected by the subway: prop up the "box"—the tube containing the subway tunnel, now exposed on its top and sides—and pour a new foundation under it, piecemeal. It can't move an inch during all this, of course, lest the tracks misalign or the walls crack. The MTA has movement gauges all over the site, and the limits are given in millimeters. One staffer involved with the project said flat out, and very much not for attribution: "They should've shut that train down for three years, and demolished the whole thing and started over." Why didn't they? It's the only train running to South Ferry and thus serving Staten Island's ferry commuters.

Piling Up Superlatives

You can pile up superlatives about the new towers from here to the 102nd floor. Two large cranes sit atop One World Trade right now, either of which can pick up 70,000 pounds in one yank. "Did you see the counterweight on the back of that thing?" Ward asks me. "It's the size of a f---ing house." The immense girders at the base of the building ("Those big pieces of steel are psycho to think about," he adds) weigh 70 tons apiece, and every one came over the George Washington Bridge and down the West Side Highway, at dawn. Altogether, 45,000 tons of structural steel will go into the first tower and 22,000 tons into the transportation hub. Much of the plaza structure is (counterintuitively) being built from the top down instead of the bottom up, because the memorial is scheduled to open before the lower concourse does. Right now, there are about 1,400 construction workers on the site, and by next year, that number will swell to 2,100. If everyone working in One World Trade were to make his way downstairs at lunch, it would take half a day, which is why there's a structure hanging inside called "the hotel": a stack of shipping containers two stories high, containing bathrooms, offices, and a Subway sandwich outlet. Every time the center of construction activity shifts, the hotel is jacked up a couple of stories.

The Port Authority is projecting an opening date of late 2013 for One World Trade and is in the process of negotiating a partial sale of the tower to a private developer. (Last week [May 9–15, 2010], the *Times* reported that Condé Nast is considering leasing up to a million square feet.) These days, a lot of what's coming into the site is concrete—up to 2,000 trucks per month, precisely timed so their contents don't start to harden before they're poured. As the job shifts from basic structure to fitting-out, deliveries become an even larger part of the logistics, because there are so many: glass, plumbing, air-conditioning ducts, all by the ton, daily. There is no vacant lot (or landfill, as was the case when the Twin Towers went up, 40-odd years ago) to stash materials, only a tiny sliver of a staging area, slotted in next to Greenwich Street. Supplies, therefore, have to arrive in small batches, just before they go into place, and over at 115 Broadway, there's an entire office devoted to coordinating trucks and deliveries. Every building site works with some kind of coordinator, but Ken Lewis, another SOM architect, explained the difference this way: "Usually, it's four guys who go over this once a week. Here it's twenty," all full-timers. (Consider all this good practice for managing the tour buses that will start streaming in after the memorial opens on the tenth anniversary of the attacks—two years before the parking garage is finished. The Port Authority is projecting that the site will be the single biggest tourist destination in America, outdrawing the Vietnam Veterans Memorial [in Washington, D.C.])

There's also another, larger trafficking group at work. Called the Lower Manhattan Construction Command Center [LMCCC], it exists to keep the whole jurisdiction circus south of Canal Street under control: forestalling clashes where, say, the Port Authority bumps into the MTA and argues with Verizon over its cables while talking to the NYPD about traffic and fielding questions from Silverstein's team. "It's certainly a challenge beyond anything the city has done before—I would say anyone has done before," says the LMCCC's executive director, Robert Harvey. "This is rebuilding a city as it operates. Everyone always says it's like doing open-heart surgery on a marathon runner in the middle of a race."

While ground zero may be an especially alluring terrorist target, we have moved into an age where every part of a major building is shaped by security plans, from truck inspections at the parking garage to airport-style screening at observation-deck gates.

When things do go a little awry, the basic nature of these buildings makes it hard to recover. Lewis lays out, just as an example, a scenario that happens all the time on your typical construction site. Let's say, after a small miscommunication between an architect and a concrete team, a wall is poured and finished, and it turns out there was supposed to be a pipe through it to carry electrical wires. In any other building, what happens next? "The contractor usually counts on being able to cut a hole in the wall afterward," Lewis explains. "Here, we have 14,000-psi [pounds per square inch] concrete"— about two and a half times denser and stronger than the usual stuff. Nobody's drilling through that. Everything has to be right the first time, and when it's not—and it sometimes isn't—undoing it is tremendously difficult.

Security: The Future of Construction

The sparkling finial that will top off One World Trade may eventually come to define it on the skyline, but extra-dense concrete is far more suggestive of what this building really is. Every inch of the tower, from subbasements on up, is braced against an imagined future attack. Its chunky base, twenty stories tall, is dramatically armored—or "hardened," the builders say. Heavy reinforced walls at street level extend outward and underground, making even the plaza explosion-resistant. The glass outer skin of One World Trade—blast-tested, successfully, out in the New Mexico desert—will hang on extra-heavy steel. That structure surrounds an inner, slightly less hefty frame that holds up floors and the rest of the interior. That, in turn, houses an elevator core, its walls up to eight feet thick, made of that super-dense concrete and packed with steel rebar as thick as your wrist. In its current raw state, it looks like the containment dome over a nuclear reactor, except with slots for turnstiles. "If we hadn't had to do that," says the Port Authority's Steve Coleman, "we'd be past 50 stories by now."

In the past, the difficulty of building in New York—even on sites as challenging as downtown Manhattan—was of local origin: the density of our urban grid, the egos of our power players, the grind of our bureaucracy. But the architecture and infrastructure of fear brings a new layer of complexity, one that stems from global forces and is largely beyond our ability to resolve. While ground zero may be an especially alluring terrorist target, we have moved into an age where every part of a major building is shaped by security plans, from truck inspections at the parking garage to airport-style screening at observation-deck gates. In this sense, One World Trade is the city's future. Asked whether he went through a background check, Gottesdiener says, "Oh, yes. Everyone does." There's a lot of stuff in that building that he can't discuss, and elements of the design that even his team of architects isn't privy to. Ask him about it, and he tightens up: "When it comes to security, we take confidentiality very seriously" is all he'll say.

2

Better Leadership Is Needed in the WTC Rebuilding Process

Glyn Vincent

Glyn Vincent is an author, playwright, and journalist.

There is a lack of progress on the World Trade Center (WTC) rebuilding project, which from the beginning has been mired in uncertainty, redesigns, court battles, and various other delays. Policy makers blame the situation on a complicated chain of command and a lack of political will and recommend an assertive, resourceful leader to pull the project together and move it forward. New Yorkers are frustrated by the lack of visible progress and are dismissive of the whole affair.

Friday is September 11th, [2009,] a day that has become our national, annual moment of truth: "Has it really been that long?" we ask ourselves. "Are we any safer or better off?" "What have we accomplished?"

In New York City, all eyes turn to ground zero our symbolic barometer of progress where the answer to the last question is inevitably, "Not much." This year after ninety-six months of starts and stops, re-designs and security modifications, court battles and other miscellaneous delays, a few steel columns of the new World Trade Center tower are finally visible, emerging from a concrete bulwark in the northwest corner of the site.

The Port Authority of New York and New Jersey has promised that the 1,776 foot-tall skyscraper (49 feet taller with the antenna than the original twin towers) will be completed in 2013 at an estimated cost of $3.1 billion. New Yorkers, though, are dubious. Many completion deadlines and budget estimates have already been blown. The *Daily News* recently cited a confidential report by the Lower Manhattan Construction Command Center (LMCCC) that warns that the tower may not be finished until 2018. Even the name of the building is mired in uncertainty. In March, the Port Authority replaced the Freedom Tower moniker with One World Trade Center, hoping that the less ideological and more practical designation would make leasing space an easier sell (they announced the change one day after signing up the building's first and, so far, only commercial lessee, Vantone Industrial Co, a Chinese enterprise).

Most of the World Trade Center site is still a vast, open lot. The Port Authority and developer Larry Silverstein are in arbitration about financing the erection of three additional office towers (the Port Authority took over the construction of the formerly called Freedom Tower in 2006), which, one report purports, will not be economically feasible until 2030. Consequently, when and how the rest of the area will be transformed into a futuristic transportation hub, shopping mall, performing arts center and September 11 museum and memorial remains, despite assurances to the contrary, largely, up in the air.

There needs to be an assertion of political leadership that demands [and] brings together the Port Authority and [developer Larry] Silverstein into the same room to work out the financing.

Better Leadership Is Needed

Councilman Alan J. Gerson, chairman of the City Council's Committee on Lower Manhattan Redevelopment, is one of those officials unhappy with the progress to date. "We should be further along," he told me. "It is unacceptable that we have lingering uncertainty about whether or not the September 11th Memorial Plaza and Museum will be completed by the 10th anniversary deadline, whether or not there will be two or three office towers built. It is totally unacceptable not to have a real specific date for the completion of these projects."

Gerson, who faces a tough reelection campaign this fall, lays much of the blame for the reconstruction delays on the multiple chains of command involved and the Port Authority. He urged Christopher Ward, executive director of the Port Authority, to issue a roadmap with specific timetables and benchmarks. Further action, Gerson went on, has to be taken. "There needs to be an assertion of political leadership that demands [and] brings together the Port Authority and [developer Larry] Silverstein into the same room to work out the financing."

The Financing Problems

The problem with that idea is that Mayor Michael Bloomberg already tried to muscle the opposing parties together in a summit meeting called last May. Representatives of Silverstein Properties, Governors David Paterson [of New York] and Jon Corzine [of New Jersey], Assembly Speaker Sheldon Silver and Port Authority officials met and decided to come up with a plan by June 11th [2009]. But they failed to agree on how to finance the construction of the buildings. Silverstein, according to a Committee on Lower Manhattan Redevelopment report, argued that frozen credit markets made raising private capital impossible and demanded more than a billion dollars in loans and guarantees from the Port Authority.

"It's all about the financing," Gerson said.

The collapse of the economy has certainly taken its toll, but what had happened to the billions in insurance money and federal aid? Gerson didn't know, but I did some research and, it turns out, most of it has already been spent, legitimately.

I suggested to the councilman that perhaps the Lower Manhattan Construction Command Center might help in the leadership arena—at least the name sounds assertive. Gerson agreed that the command center was a possibility, but that it was funded by and reporting to too many bosses. "To be effective they need to be more established—a fully funded, independent watch dog," he said. "What this site needs is a sheriff."

[Wild West sheriff Wild Bill] Hickok or none, New Yorkers, accustomed to seeing a corner deli replaced by a forty story residential tower in a matter of months, are understandably dismissive of the whole affair. "It's a political football," Liz Nevin, a born and bred in New York friend of mine, scoffed. "It will never get done in our lifetime." Most of America hopes she's wrong.

3

The World Trade Center Rebuild Is a National Disgrace

Keith B. Richburg

Keith B. Richburg is a foreign correspondent for the Washington Post.

Political infighting, endless delays, redesigns, and court battles have characterized the rebuilding of the World Trade Center site, which has become a political nightmare. According to many observers, the project is too ambitious and the design and construction hindered by too many legal, economic, and political constraints to be as impressive as many Americans want it to be.

In the aftermath of the Sept. 11, 2001, attacks, with the ruins of the World Trade Center still smoldering, political leaders from New York Mayor Rudolph W. Giuliani to President George W. Bush vowed to quickly rebuild the site, bigger and better than before.

"The skyline will be made whole again," Giuliani said. And as a sign of the city's resilience, initial plans called for the rebuilding to be complete by 2011—the 10th anniversary of the terrorist attacks.

Eight years later [in 2009], the site known as Ground Zero remains mostly a giant hole in the ground. A projected completion date has been pushed back years, if not decades. The project has been beset by repeated delays, changing designs, billions of dollars in cost overruns, and feuding among the various parties involved in the complex undertaking.

"It's just one big political nightmare," said Jim Riches, a retired New York deputy fire chief, who lost his firefighter son, Jimmy, on 9/11 and who has attended meetings on the progress of the construction. "I think it's a national disgrace," he said. "I really think it's horrible. We can put a man on the moon, but we can't get all the politicians in New York . . . to build the World Trade Center back up again."

Rebuilding the World Trade Center site was always going to be an extremely complex undertaking.

Visions and Realities

What happened over the past eight years is a story of grandiose plans clashing with practical realities; of the flush of early emotions giving way to cold, financial calculus; of public officials fighting with a private developer; and of bureaucrats battling one another at almost every level with no one really in charge.

"Nobody wants to accept responsibility," said former New York Mayor Edward I. Koch. He joined others in laying blame before two chief agencies: the Port Authority of New York and New Jersey, which owns the land, and the Lower Manhattan Development Corp., which was created to channel all federal aid pouring in. "It's shameful that they have failed in their responsibility to build this in a measured and responsible way," Koch said.

A sad symbol of the slow progress is the former Deutsche Bank building, next to where the twin towers stood. The 40-story building was heavily damaged by the collapse of the World Trade Center's South Tower and was declared uninhabitable. Eight years later, the building still has not been torn down: Two firefighters died in a blaze in the building in 2007, suspending the deconstruction, and the discovery of toxic dust inside—with asbestos, lead and other dangerous chemicals—has caused further delays.

A Complicated Project

Rebuilding the World Trade Center site was always going to be an extremely complex undertaking. At 16 acres, the site is larger than the downtown of many other American cities. It sits atop the intersection of several major city subway lines and a commuter train line to New Jersey. Its location in a densely packed part of Lower Manhattan makes it difficult for construction crews to work, while its proximity to City Hall, police headquarters and the federal courts prompts security concerns.

The initial reaction after the attacks was to rebuild the twin towers exactly as they were before, as a show of defiance to the terrorists. But some family members—many of whom were never able to retrieve the remains of their loved ones from the dust—insisted that the footprints of the original towers be left untouched, out of respect for those who died.

Residents of Lower Manhattan and developers, meanwhile, envisioned adding retail shops to the vast expanse of office space that made up the towers.

Changes in Plans

A 2005 design called for a spiraling glass skyscraper, named Freedom Tower, that would rise a symbolic 1,776 feet in the air. But after the design was unveiled, the New York Police Department said the new building would be too vulnerable to truck-bomb attacks and sent the architects back to the drawing board. A redesign moved the tower back from the street and placed it atop an impregnable 200-foot steel-and-concrete base.

Then, this year the name was changed to World Trade Center One, out of concern that Freedom Tower would become too tempting a target for terrorism.

The ambitious plan now calls for four office towers, including World Trade Center One, with a memorial and two tree-lined reflecting pools standing on the footprints where the old twin towers stood. Cascading waterfalls lead down to a museum, 70 feet below ground level. The plan also includes a massive futuristic-looking transportation hub to rival Grand Central Terminal.

By some estimates, the entire project involves more than a dozen government agencies and at least 100 construction companies and subcontractors.

Financial Issues

The projected costs have soared far above the $15 billion budget, construction is years behind schedule, and Larry Silverstein, the developer of three towers, is locked in a dispute over financing with the Port Authority.

Silverstein wants the Port Authority to back loans to build two of the towers. He has blamed the authority's delays for costing him crucial financing, since private support became hard to find after credit markets froze [in 2008]. The matter recently went to arbitration.

As time has passed since the 2001 attacks, some are now questioning the complexity of the plan.

Leadership Is Needed

Alan J. Gerson, the City Council member whose district includes Ground Zero, said, "We're mad as hell, and getting madder at the prospect of additional delay." He said that "the site needs a sheriff" to oversee the various agencies, troubleshoot, mediate disputes, and solve engineering and financial problems.

Mayor Michael R. Bloomberg tried unsuccessfully over the summer to mediate the dispute between Silverstein and the Port Authority. He later issued a tough statement that blasted the impasse and the resulting delay as "unacceptable" and "intolerable," saying, "This cannot continue." Bloomberg would like a larger say in determining Ground Zero's fate, but the city's role is limited.

Other Factors

As time has passed since the 2001 attacks, some are now questioning the complexity of the plan. Others are wondering whether a city hit hard by the recession—with a shrunken financial sector and with a glut of cheap commercial space—really needs to be spending billions to add 9 million more square feet of office space. A report commissioned by the [Port] Authority estimates that it will be 2030 before all the space can be filled.

"The design of that site was done in a political and emotional environment," said Kathryn Wylde, president of the Partnership for New York City, a nonprofit business group. "It wasn't realistic about the technical aspects and the cost, and it wasn't realistic about anticipating that this was a long-term project that would have to go through changes.

"All of America wanted to show our resilience," Wylde said. "As time has gone by, it's become increasingly clear that we can fight back and show our resilience and strength, but we have to do it within the constraints of how much we have to spend."

4

A Revised Plan Has Gotten the World Trade Center Rebuild Back on Track

Scott Raab

Scott Raab is a writer and a contributing journalist for Esquire.

Great progress has been made on the World Trade Center rebuilding project in the past few years, compared with 2005 when daunting delays and political infighting resulted in inertia and uncertainty. The difference has been effective leadership and a political will to get the job done. Since Chris Ward of the Port Authority of New York and New Jersey took the lead in 2008 there has been a marked improvement in morale and progress.

I'll tell you this about New York City during the summer of the Ground Zero mosque here in year nine [2010] of our nation's engagement in the holy war triggered by Osama bin Laden [leader of terrorist organization al Qaeda] and now affixed to Orwellian [referring to the writings of George Orwell] permanence: It's hot—ungodly hot—the woolen air a haze clinging to every pore. This morning brought a downpour not long after dawn that felt less like relief than ten minutes slumped against the wall of a shvitz [steambath] getting pissed on by goats. Not that I'd know.

"You don't mind the air conditioner, do ya?" Lenny laughs, planting himself behind the wheel of the truck. He's hauling concrete from Brooklyn to the World Trade Center work site in downtown Manhattan.

"This is ten yards on board," Lenny says. "This is a twelve-yard truck with normal concrete—a sidewalk mix, whatever. This is twelve thousand PSI, much heavier a mix, much looser. That's why we only carry ten yards."

Delivering Concrete

The worlds within the worlds within the world of concrete? Forget about it. I can tell you that a yard of concrete is twenty-seven cubic feet—the volume of concrete sufficient to fill a cube measuring three feet by three feet; that after thousands of years—the Egyptians used concrete to build the pyramids—it still takes a mix of water, sand, stone, and cement to make up a batch of concrete; that adding substances—a whole range of chemicals and industrial by-products—to the mix changes the properties of the concrete to fit the job it needs to do; that while fire and the wheel get the glory, civilization uses more concrete than any other man-made substance. I can tell you that much of the concrete poured at the World Trade Center is the heaviest, strongest concrete ever poured anywhere. And I can tell you that Lenny has under ninety minutes from the time his truck is filled to deliver his ten yards to the site.

Actually, Lenny's the guy who can tell you all that, not me. But Lenny grew up in Brooklyn, a neighborhood called East New York, and lives in Staten Island now, and his accent is thick. In fact, everything about Lenny is thick, including his passenger this morning, me. Between us and the concrete, this truck's going eighty thousand pounds, give or take.

Except that the truck's not going anywhere. We're stuck in the two-mile long Brooklyn Battery Tunnel, the world's longest underwater traffic tunnel, and by stuck I mean stopped cold in the morning rush hour. The only thing moving is the drum of concrete spinning slow behind us, keeping its load loose.

"Backed up in the tunnel?" Lenny says after five standstill minutes. "Have some Ex-Lax."

Sour dills do it for me.

A Daily Routine

"It's like [comedian] Groucho Marx said—a clown's like an aspirin but twice as fast. That's how you feel sometimes when you go up to the Trade Center. You know what happened there, but you kid around and the humor helps you out."

It's a six-mile circuit from where the trucks load, hard by the Gowanus Canal, to the work site. They start loading a little after 6:00 AM and hit the truck route ten minutes or so apart. There's a 260-yard pour at Tower 4—we're in the middle of that now—and a smaller pour at the memorial in the early afternoon. Other concrete companies are pouring Tower 1 and the new train station.

"Not for nothing," Lenny says, "but they used to have booths here—the cops used to stay inside the booths. No longer. Today you got modern technology. That's it"—one thick finger jabbing high on the windshield—"right there in the ceiling. Cameras everywhere. Everywhere you go."

We all right timewise?

"We'll be okay on the time. The job is close enough where even if you lose a half hour you're still in good shape. Unless you're really warming up."

Delivery Like Clockwork

Whatever the weather, concrete produces its own heat as the water and the cement bond; on a morning like this, each batch mixed in the central drum that fills the trucks includes enough ice—shredded and blown into the mix from three-hundred-pound blocks kept frozen in a trailer nearby—to get it down to 65 degrees or so when it's loaded.

"Without the ice," Lenny says, "it'd be in the low 80s. The customer wants it to be 75 degrees. No problem."

Fifteen, twenty minutes, the tunnel loosens up, and we bounce into lower Manhattan. The spotter at the gate at the northwest corner of Ground Zero sees Lenny a block and a half away, sitting above a long row of cars at a red light.

"See to the left? He's washin' truck 84—78 should be at the pump now. The guy out in the street there"—that'd be the spotter—"he saw this truck. He just told him I'm here. He's dumpin' him out. He's gonna empty out that truck so they're gonna be ready when I get in there. It's like a drive-through here. Watch this."

Sure enough. By the time we reach the site, 84 is on its way back to the tunnel, 78 is getting cleaned up, and Lenny has 103 backed up under one of the Tower 4 pumps ready to take his load up to the crew pouring another floor.

"That's Tony Junior," Lenny says. "He's in charge. That's Good-Lookin' Pete right there. Guy to the left, his name is Larry—he's the Teamster steward on the job."

The Working Crew

It's a tight-knit bunch, although—for the record—Pete isn't really looking all that good this morning. A lot of these guys go back together before 9/11—in New York City, the construction business is a very small world—but the shared experience of that cataclysmic day and its aftermath cured and hardened their bond into something like concrete.

"I realized the other day—I was talking to one of the contractors who was there, too, all that time—I said, 'You know, we've been here almost ten years now.'"

Lenny shakes his head, remembering.

"Thousands of people—I remember we had to shore up Church Street. The fire underground—they had steel plates across Church and Liberty—it was all torn up. Sitting in the trucks, waiting to go into the site, the heat underground, it actually melted the tires off the steel—three, four months after. I'll never, ever, ever forget that smell. Never. I'll never forget how it smelled."

A Troubled History

I got here five years ago, in the spring of 2005, long after the smell was gone. I'll never forget how it looked: barren, battered, bereft, a broken place sitting seventy feet below street level, with one long ramp running down into it. Three empty construction trailers, a couple of old beams waiting to be trucked up the ramp, and two large squares outlined by orange construction cones marking the footprints of the fallen Twin Towers. A cornerstone—boxed in wood, sitting in a pool of rainwater, nothing but a politician's prop—for a building that would never be built.

What you never had at Ground Zero was the one and only thing that was ever going to make a difference—the thing that you have there now: effective leadership of an actual construction project.

By then—nearly four years after 9/11—it had become clear that no one was in charge at Ground Zero. You had a landlord—the Port Authority of New York and New Jersey, which owns these sixteen acres and built the World Trade Center—and a tenant fighting for control of the property; you had dueling architects; you had a state agency created by Rudy Giuliani before he left the mayor's office designed specifically to keep a fellow Republican, Governor George E. Pataki, in charge of the funding and planning of rebuilding; you had community boards and groups of folks who'd lost loved ones on 9/11 and local and national politicians and the Port Authority and the tenant and editorial writers and architects all locked in endless tugs-of-war over what should be built, when and by whom, and who was to blame for the resulting impasse.

You had, in short, a pit, variously described as a hole in the ground and in the city's heart, a national disgrace, an insult to the 9/11 dead, and proof that the terrorists had won.

You had promises that weren't kept, deadlines that weren't met, villains on all sides.

What you never had at Ground Zero was the one and only thing that was ever going to make a difference—the thing that you have there now: effective leadership of an actual construction project.

The Scope of the Project

A living layer cake of building—four superskyscrapers, a memorial plaza atop a museum, a transit hub, a subway line, each at a different stage, all separate yet inseparable.

It is, in toto, vast. The size and noise of it hit you in the face as soon as you're within the gates. You need earplugs, water to cut the dust in your mouth and throat. It's too big to see when it's all in front of you. You need a guide.

On a good day at Ground Zero—and they've all been good days for some time now—it's a hoe-ram symphony, a crane ballet, a three-dimensional tribute to patience, pure grit, and engineering genius.

But Lenny can take you only so far. Where Lenny's truck has dumped its concrete is at the southeast corner of the site, where Tower 4 is beginning to rise above the stump of its base. Crews are beginning foundation work for Towers 2 and 3; both sit due north of 4, in a row that descends from the crew pouring concrete for the twentieth floor of T4 down to the excavators sitting seventy feet below street level at what will become the base of Tower 2.

That's only one slice. The subway line, the transit hub— the train station known hereabouts simply as the Calatrava [after its designer]—and a portion of the street-level plaza form another slice, just west of the row of towers.

The other slice—roughly half of the site—consists of the memorial and Tower 1. At street level, the memorial will be a pair of fountains—each a waterfall of thirty feet—within the footprints of the Twin Towers, lined by parapets etched with the names of the victims of 9/11 and set off within the site by a maze of trees and walks.

This is all happening right now, in real time, and it's enough to make a patriot's heart thump. On a good day at Ground Zero—and they've all been good days for some time now—it's a hoe-ram symphony, a crane ballet, a three-dimensional tribute to patience, pure grit, and engineering genius.

So tell me: How come all these asshats are still calling it just a hole in the ground?

A New Leader

"This is the one that pissed me off," says Chris Ward, executive director of the Port Authority [PA] of New York and New Jersey, owner of these sixteen acres. "Newt Gingrich, on the front page of *The New York Times*, is quoted on the mosque issue: 'We're gonna allow the Muslims to build it within two blocks of Ground Zero, where we haven't built anything.'"

Ward's our guide today, and the dress shirt under his screaming-green safety vest makes him no less a Ground Zero warrior-hero. The Port's purview includes all the major bridges, tunnels, and airports connecting New York City to the world; Ward's in charge of six thousand employees and a multibillion-dollar annual budget, and he answers to the New York and New Jersey politicians who traditionally have used the PA as a cash cow, patronage pit, and whipping boy.

Ward's immediate predecessors were hacks—Pataki's puppet was a guy from upstate New York who once ran his family's car wash and bowling alley—who mainly hid from public view while the boss overpromised and underdelivered. Ward, a barrel-chested egghead whose résumé includes a master's in theology from Harvard's divinity school, is a straight-shooting leader.

A Practical Assessment of the Project

Within weeks of his appointment as the Port Authority's executive director in May 2008, Chris Ward did something no less heroic for being necessary: He called bullshit on the whole damned thing. At the behest of New York Governor David Paterson—who hired Ward after inheriting the governorship from the crusading whoremonger Eliot Spitzer—he delivered a thirty-four-page report that boiled down to this: Ground Zero's budget and deadlines were so at odds with reality that it would take three months more just to figure out a realistic schedule to finish the rebuilding.

"Myopic monumentalism wrecked this project," Ward says. "You can't have a monument in a day. You don't define the project by that at the beginning. You have to build it—and that requires patience. It requires hard work, and it requires deadlines.

"We know every single day how much steel has to be placed, and how much concrete has to be poured, and we are driving every contractor for that level of completion. It is getting done.

"And let's just step back here. We've done a lot—we've built 700,000 square feet below grade [underground], we're building an air-conditioning system for 1.8 million square feet of public space. It's a kids' game of pickup sticks—they're tied together. You can't touch one without touching everything else.

"We'll go down in the PATH [Port Authority Trans-Hudson, a rapid transit railroad] station so you can see the open-heart surgery that's going on to keep the PATH trains running while we're tearing down the platforms."

The PATH Station

Through an unmarked door inside the temporary PATH station—the railroad loops through the site, toting tens of thousands of commuters around the clock and seven days a week from New Jersey—and down, with Ward in the lead, into another world framed in steel and concrete, lit by bulbs hung from metal poles, mapped by countless plywood pathways laid by countless work crews as, day by day, they build a new World Trade Center from the ground up.

"Look at that," Ward says as a PATH train shrieks past. "That train curves and you're about six inches from the new shear wall that we're literally now pouring."

Once the train passes, we walk toward the center of the site, through a maze of utility work—in addition to public space, the rebuilt Trade Center will host ten million square feet of office space—and pump rooms.

"That gray steel over there is the floor of the foundation," says Ward. "We're gonna bring it all the way over to the top here. So while there's still work being done down here, the PATH station ceiling will be there—more importantly, the floor of the memorial'll be there, so we can plant the trees and finish the fountains. We're building from the top down."

The Memorial Pavilion

This is a point of great pride with Ward and the Port Authority engineers: In order to get the memorial ready for the tenth anniversary of 9/11, they redesigned the job and turned it upside down, so the memorial pavilion—the plaza that itself forms part of the PATH station's ceiling—can be built first.

"You can't say the memorial's the most important thing, so put your shovel down and let's wait on the transit hub. The mechanical systems that drive the memorial fountains, the air-conditioning, and the lighting for the memorial are in the basement of the hub. So I had a difficult conversation with Santiago [Calatrava]. He's not used to difficult conversations—it was hard to get a word in edgewise—but we made it clear that he is building to an owner, not to himself."

Here Ward grins. Santiago Calatrava is an international superstar, a consummate artist, an engineer as well as an architect, and he had designed—to universal acclaim—a stunning hall entirely free of columns, all space and light, clasped by ribs of curving white concrete. It was an engineering marvel and, at the original budget of $2 billion, the most expensive train station ever built.

A Turning Point

But once it became clear that both the cost and the complexity of building it were going to bust the budget and the rebuilding timetable, Ward had no choice but to ask for a sitdown with Calatrava. He could not have felt comfortable as a nickel-nursing, git-er-done politburo hack putting the squeeze on Santiago. But that's precisely what Ward did, and he looks back at that fondly as one of the rebuilding's turning points.

"Literally, right here, is where all of these backspans and trusses are gonna be, and the way he designed them, you literally had to bring them in and drop them, and the steel would bend to a point and form where it was supposed to be. But that could've been incredibly costly and risky if you had to keep placing it. This huge truss that goes down the middle of the Calatrava hub—the thing is like welding forty plates together because it holds up the whole ceiling.

"He came to the table with some very, very creative ways of solving a lot of the construction complexity. So we've done four columns. You can't even really tell they're there."

Crossing the site toward Tower 1 in the far northwest corner, we climb a few wood stairs until we reach a level even with the memorial footprints.

"That's the lower void of the South Tower. Look at these pumps. Sixty thousand gallons a minute for the memorial. The pavilion is almost overhead—instead of building from the bottom up, we flipped the memorial staging structure so the memorial will be done by the ten-year anniversary.

The voids where the Twin Towers stood have long been Ground Zero's spiritual center.

"We'll have the fountains working, the names on the parapets of those who were lost, and 80 percent of the trees fully planted.

"We made a commitment to the mayor, we made a commitment to the two governors—that memorial will be done on the ten-year anniversary. That's the only thing that matters."

From Ward's lips to God's ears: If the Port Authority can't get that much finished by 9/11/11, it may be his last day on the job. And he knows it.

Honoring the Lost

The voids where the Twin Towers stood have long been Ground Zero's spiritual center. When the site was cleared of debris, they immediately were declared off-limits to vehicles and equipment, and they have retained a certain solemnity throughout the rebuilding. The crews lining their floors and walls with black granite wear black hard hats, which seem to be impossible to obtain for the not-so-few collectors among the rebuilding throng.

It is artisanal work, befitting its character and purpose.

Nobody will forget that this patch of land—as wrenched by dispute as any in the world—also is, literally, a mass grave.

For that very reason, many voices—among them, in his mayoral farewell address, Rudy Giuliani's—argued that the entire site should become a vast memorial. That this idea failed to gain any real traction says at least as much about New York City's—and America's—fighting spirit, resilience, and self-security as it says about the worth of real estate in Manhattan.

But the memorial is no less vital for that, and it is—even now, in its infancy—breathtaking.

"Come on," Ward says. "Let's go over to 1 World."

That's what the Port Authority has renamed the Freedom Tower. So far, no good: Everyone else still calls it the Freedom Tower.

"We're just about to hit the standard floor, which means every floor plate is like the one on top of it, so the guys can get some momentum going and start punching 'em out. By this year's anniversary, we should be around fifty or fifty-five, and then by the ten-year anniversary, we should be topped out at ninety."

Looking Back to 2005

On my first trip to the pit, in '05, I met Marc Becker.

"I know it's gonna happen," Becker told me then, speaking of the tower finally rising. "I just don't know when."

I could almost hear his teeth grinding as he said it. His blue Tishman hard hat—Tishman construction helped put up the old Twin Towers, and it's running the Tower 1 job for the Port Authority now—was covered with stickers, his 9/11 battle ribbons, marking him as a veteran of the rescue and recovery efforts. He was patient with my questions, all nuts-and-bolts stuff about pumping water out of the pit and figuring out how to build a skyscraper's foundation around a working railroad track, but I could see him getting flushed as I kept trying to make sense of construction basics that were second nature to him.

"All I can tell ya is we're ready to build," he said finally. "We're ready to go. It's very personal to me. It's not just a job."

Seeing the Difference

Back then, nearly a year after Pataki had dedicated a cornerstone, crews were still waiting for the Port Authority, the architects, and the NYPD [New York Police Department] to figure out how to secure 1 World Trade's base.

"It's personal. It's personal. I saw all the horrors. I mean horrors. From day one."

And then he choked up and couldn't talk anymore.

Now we're sitting in a small construction trailer fifty yards from Tower 1, at street level. Through the small rectangular window, the titanic seventy-foot trusses rise at its base, painted with a dull red epoxy, awaiting fireproofing.

Above—day by day, a floor a week—750 men are busy raising Tower 1.

5

There Should Be Twin Towers Instead of One World Trade Center

Nicole Gelinas

Nicole Gelinas is a City Journal *contributing editor and the Searle Freedom Trust Fellow at the Manhattan Institute.*

It is not too late to replace the single Freedom Tower on the World Trade Center site with twin towers, which would be more modern and sleek than the ones that were destroyed by terrorist attacks in 2001. This is a common sense solution, because it would offer a poignant tribute to the old buildings, as well as lower costs. Two towers instead of one would also have a symbolic significance.

Since al-Qaida [terrorist organization] demolished the World Trade Center nearly seven years ago, New York's naked emperors—Governors George Pataki and Eliot Spitzer and architect Daniel Libeskind—have viewed an historic rebuilding challenge as an opportunity to invent a square wheel and then deny for years that it can't roll. This week [July 2008], the Port Authority [of New York and New Jersey], which runs the site, released a report admitting that little progress had been made there—still more evidence that the government has responded to an external attack with a self-inflicted disaster. But all the dillydallying may provide an unlikely opportunity for [New York] Governor David Paterson and World Trade Center developer Larry Silverstein, who should examine an entirely different approach: building new twin towers at Ground Zero.

Little Progress

It may sound crazy to say that we should consider throwing away years' worth of planning. But we've barely moved toward completion since 2002; in fact, last week's report threw out cost estimates or timetables for rebuilding. "The schedule and cost for each of the public projects on the site face significant delays and cost overruns," wrote Chris Ward, the new director of the Port Authority, to Paterson last Monday. Further, "at least 15 fundamental issues critical to the overall project" are "not yet . . . resolved."

New twin towers wouldn't be the old ones; nobody can pretend that 9/11 never happened.

Indeed: all New York has to show for its hoping and waiting is a partial support structure for the Freedom Tower—which, when it's built, will be a sad white elephant. And all that the state promises today is more waiting: waiting for officials to figure out how a poorly designed, half-billion-dollar memorial can withstand the weight of the trees that are supposed to go on top of it; waiting for them to figure out a workable plan for the fancy, multibillion-dollar, [Santiago] Calatrava-designed transit hub, where inevitable changes will mean more changes and delays to everything else on the site. Can anyone be confident that the eventual results won't be physical evidence of unimaginable folly?

New York City Needs Twin Towers

On 9/11 [2001], al-Qaida murdered 2,974 people and destroyed two iconic office towers that dominated New York's skyline, another lone office tower nearby, and some smaller support buildings. We can't recover stolen lives. But what would it take to make New York physically whole again, while paying tribute to 9/11's history and victims? One obvious answer is to build two iconic office towers that dominate New York's skyline once again, surrounded by some smaller buildings. Notice that the one project that has achieved completion after 9/11—Silverstein's Seven World Trade Center, the lone office tower near the main site—did so partly because Silverstein realized that al-Qaida's attack wasn't a mandate to reinvent the obvious. He simply built a more elegant tower to succeed what al-Qaida had destroyed, modernized for the twenty-first century in terms of safety and aesthetics and placed in a superior setting.

New York could take a similar approach with the rest of the site. New twin towers wouldn't be the old ones; nobody can pretend that 9/11 never happened. They'd offer modern, sleek designs, as Seven World Trade Center does, and they'd be built to private-sector specifications. They'd need twenty-first-century, post-9/11 safety upgrades. The site would also need an appropriate memorial and well-designed public spaces.

It may not be too late to take this commonsense approach to rebuilding, which was never the puzzle the world's great architects have made it out to be. For a truly breathtaking example of what New York *could* achieve at Ground Zero, take a look at what the late Herb Belton, an architect who worked on the original twin towers, and structural engineer Ken Gardner have proposed. Gardner, working first with Belton and then on his own since Belton died in 2005, has come up with twin towers that do far more than recreate the originals. "Using the original blueprints, [we've] re-engineered the design to recapture the Towers' greatness, while diligently addressing their flaws," Gardner says. "As a result, the design incorporates robust security, construction economy, and the greenest technology. The retail space is inviting, the commercial space is exceptional, and the outdoor spaces are a pedestrian-friendly oasis." Gardner, always flexible, surely wouldn't mind tweaks to his proposed towers so that they pay homage to the old ones without coming too close to replicating them. He also proposes that state officials allow residential condos in one of the new towers, as in the successful Time Warner Center, another set of twin towers uptown.

A Common Sense Design

Gardner's proposed memorial makes intuitive sense. It would preserve the destroyed towers' footprints—the new towers would be built opposite them—while evoking their famous facades. He'd restore the now-damaged bronze globe sculpture that used to sit outside the towers, with 88 flags surrounding it to represent the nations that lost citizens on 9/11; he'd also offer a simple garden for quiet reflection. Such a poignant tribute would be a vast improvement on what's planned. As my colleague Steven Malanga has written, smaller memorials to 9/11 victims elsewhere often focus on images of the twin towers, yet the memorial now planned for the actual site, a strange amalgam of water and trees, is sadly generic and irrelevant.

Does it serve anyone if the nation gradually forgets what used to stand at Ground Zero?

A simpler, intuitive design could mean lower costs over the construction period and lower costs to maintain the buildings as well. Gardner thinks that one of his towers could sit on the foundation already partly built for the Freedom Tower and that the materials the Port Authority has ordered for the Freedom Tower could be used at one of the other building sites. He also says that the state could build the memorial by the tenth anniversary of 9/11, a promise officials can't make today. Financing will be a challenge, sure, but as New York undergoes a financial-industry meltdown, it will be no matter what we build.

Safety Concerns

As for people who think that no one would lease space or go to work in new twin towers, they forget that the new towers wouldn't be the same as the old ones. They'd look different, and people would feel differently about them, just as is the case with the new Seven World Trade Center. The only benefit of the delay so far, in fact, is that emotions have subsided and fears have receded, allowing us to consider, at least, building new twin towers. Yes, terrorist attacks would be a risk, but that would be the case whatever we built at Ground Zero, as continuing concerns over the site's security plans show. People ride on subways and bridges, and work in other high-profile towers, despite the risk of terrorism.

Gardner answers understandable fear with hope. He notes that new towers rising in the skyline—something that he thinks is possible within little more than a year, if the state could get its act together—would uplift New Yorkers. "There is nothing to suggest that the current design could ever hope to enjoy a similar success," he adds. Think, too, of the little kids you see today wandering around the site's perimeter with their parents. They're far too young to remember the twin towers. Does it serve anyone if the nation gradually forgets what used to stand at Ground Zero?

Of course, Silverstein, the private leaseholder, must make the ultimate decision about what's commercially viable at the part of the site he controls. But Silverstein didn't freely draw up the current office-tower designs; they were the best he could do under the bizarre constraints that Pataki and Libeskind foisted on him. He, along with Governor Paterson, should take this invaluable opportunity at least to reconsider.

If there's a chance of making a more elegant choice, the two men should be bold in saying so. They may be surprised at the public's reaction.

6

Changing the Name of the Freedom Tower Is Controversial

Margaret Schmidt

Margaret Schmidt is the managing editor of the Jersey Journal.

Naming the tower being built at the World Trade Center site "Freedom Tower" was symbolic. Changing the name to One World Trade Center has provoked a firestorm of controversy, as critics accuse the Port Authority of New York and New Jersey of being unpatriotic. Supporters of the name change, however, point to security concerns as well as the necessity for marketing commercial space to high-profile clients.

Even without the name, the symbolism of the Freedom Tower as an American response to the Sept. 11 [2001] terror attacks was hard to miss.

The original architect designed a twisting form he wanted to imitate the Statue of Liberty, with a spire that rose to the deliberate height of 1,776 feet (541 meters) to recognize the year of American independence. Politicians called the tower proof of the country's triumph over terrorism.

Former New York Gov. George Pataki said visitors to the iconic skyscraper "will know our determination to overcome evil" in a 2003 speech that first gave the Freedom Tower its name.

A Name Change

The tower—still under construction with a projected completion date of 2013—no longer has the same architect, design or footprint on the 16-acre (6.5-hectare) site. And this week [March 22–28, 2009], the owners of Ground Zero publicly parted ways with the Freedom Tower name, saying it would be more practical to market the tallest building in New York as the former north tower's name, One World Trade Center.

Critics called the name drop an unpatriotic shedding of symbolism by the Port Authority of New York and New Jersey. Some newspaper editorials blasted the agency for years of missed deadlines and changing plans for the site.

"When you've broken your promises on everything else to do with redeveloping ground zero, it's no big deal to discard the name by which the public has come to know the iconic skyscraper at the heart of the plan," the *New York Daily News* wrote yesterday.

Reasoning Behind the Renaming

But others privately repeated fears that have plagued the building as negotiations with major corporations to take up space in the tower came and went: that the 102-story Freedom Tower's name could make it more susceptible to future attacks than a symbol of defiance against it.

"The fact is, more than 3 billion dollars of public money is invested in that building and, as a public agency, we have the responsibility to make sure it is completed and that we utilize the best strategy to make certain it is fully occupied," the Port Authority said in a statement yesterday.

Agency chairman Anthony Coscia was more critical in remarks Thursday, when the Port Authority announced its first corporate lease at the tower with a Chinese business center.

"As we market the building, we will ensure the building is presented in the best possible way," he said. One World Trade

Center is "easiest for people to identify with, and frankly, we've gotten a very interested and warm reception to it."

Security Concerns

Coscia had expressed concerns about the Freedom Tower three years earlier, saying he would never ask Port Authority employees to move into the tallest, most symbolic skyscraper being built at the site because they had survived 1993 and 2001 terrorist attacks and would find it too emotionally difficult to return.

Several other government offices were located in the original trade center, and the Port Authority is trying to finalize leases with the federal and state governments that would lease half the building. No other corporate tenants have signed on. The Port Authority has agreed to lease space in another tower being built at the site.

More Controversy

Pataki—who named the Freedom Tower in his 2003 speech and continued to refer to it in rebuilding speeches as a symbol of America's ability to come back after Sept. 11, took offense at the loss of the Freedom Tower moniker and its replacement.

"Where One and Two World Trade Center once stood, there will be a memorial with two voids to honor the heroes we lost. In my view, those addresses should never be used again," he said.

The Daily News and *New York Post* published editorials backing the former governor. But *The New York Times* wrote today that Pataki's name for the building became "its burden," and said the Port Authority was "quietly and sensibly" using another name to market the tower to high-profile commercial tenants.

The Port Authority suggested that people could still call the building the Freedom Tower; the name has stuck despite the fact that the agency quietly stopped it on first reference years ago. The agency made One World Trade Center the building's legal name when it took over its construction in 2006, although it also acquired the trademark for the Freedom Tower name.

[New York] Mayor Michael Bloomberg—who said yesterday he prefers the name Freedom Tower—said the building's true name may be left to the public.

"One of the things is we call things what we want to call them. So Avenue of Americas is a good example. It's Sixth Avenue to most people," the mayor said. "If they name this One World Trade Center, people will still call it the Freedom Tower."

7

The World Trade Center Site Is Not Hallowed Ground

Jack Shafer

Jack Shafer is a writer for Slate, *an online magazine.*

The World Trade Center site is not hallowed ground, which is a religious concept; since the United States is not a religious state, the term does not apply. In fact, it is a commercial site. All talk about the site as hallowed ground is cover for political maneuvering and attempts to manipulate the collective memories of the attacks for political purposes.

Every year, the custody battle over 9/11 becomes more contentious. The current [2010] furor over the proposed construction of an Islamic center a couple of blocks away from the World Trade Center [WTC] footprint has made this anniversary of the carnage at the towers, the Pentagon, and Shanksville, Pa., more prickly than usual.

Claiming Ownership of 9/11

New Yorkers have thought from the beginning that the calamity belongs to them because, well, because they're egocentrics who think that everything belongs to them. But New Yorkers would also have you believe that the day belongs to them because their city endured the greatest fatalities. (The Jerseyites who died? Fuggedaboutit.) Those who lost relatives in the attacks tend to think of 9/11 as their personal property because their immediate loss was so great. But that doesn't mean they see eye to eye about everything 9/11. Some would have liked to see the WTC site sculpted into a "cemetery" or permanent memorial. Others thought their special status should have given them a louder voice in dictating the size, shape, and use of any replacement buildings. Today, September Eleventh Families for Peaceful Tomorrows sings "Kumbaya" as they encourage alternatives to war and attempt to build universal fellowship. The September 11th Education Trust, which started as a family group, seeks to preserve the day with oral histories and archival materials. Meanwhile, 9/11 Families for a Safe & Strong America takes a hard line and is currently protesting the building of the Islamic center.

Politics of 9/11

Politicians claimed ownership of 9/11 almost from the get-go to advance their goals. Within five hours of the strike, Secretary of Defense Donald H. Rumsfeld was plotting ways to harness it as an excuse to attack Iraq. The [George W.] Bush administration and Congress invoked 9/11 as they rushed into law in six weeks an act composed largely of a police- and surveillance-powers wish list they had been keeping on a shelf, which they dubbed the USA PATRIOT Act. And, of course, the Bush administration repeatedly conjured images of 9/11 over the next 20 months to successfully campaign for the Iraq invasion.

New York Mayor Rudolph Giuliani grabbed 9/11's pink slip before the dust had even settled. President George W. Bush rushed to the site to wave the flag and hug the firefighters. New York's Republican Gov. George Pataki spent more than one-third of his 2002 State of the State address talking about 9/11, according to the *Albany Times Union*, which came in an election year for Pataki. When Pataki challenger Andrew Cuomo claimed that the governor had merely "held the leader's [Giuliani's] coat" and not led after the attack, Republicans went insane on Cuomo, and newspaper editorials denounced him for needlessly politicizing the day!

Owning the Wind

Claiming ownership of a day is a little like claiming ownership of the wind. Nobody can prevent you from staking your claim, but getting your hands on the deed usually proves impossible. Ordinarily, Americans sort out these historical property disputes by ignoring their differences. That's what Northerners and Southerners eventually did about the Civil War, um, I mean the War Between the States. Although the two factions may still disagree vehemently about the war's causes and its prosecution, they're united in their interest in the war's history and its battlefields. So they've politely agreed to share custody. More recent American epochs, like Labor Day, Memorial Day, and Dec. 7 [the day in 1941 that the Japanese attacked Pearl Harbor], have been bled of any strife and most of their import over time. Independence Day is the best example. It's long been more about time off work, cookouts, and fireworks than about liberty.

The sharpest example of this sort of holiday erosion can be found in Martin Luther King Jr. Day, which has been observed as a federal holiday since 1986. Although much argued over when adopted and not embraced by all states until recent years, it's now as dull and mainstream as tap water. While still a supersignificant day for some, its strict observance has waned. In a decade or two, maybe King Day will become something like Presidents Day or Memorial Day—a noteworthy holiday but also an occasion for free curbside-parking and shopping.

The Myth of Hallowed Ground

How far away can 9/11 sales at department stores be? Pretty far, I would guess, because too many people still regard 9/11 as a religious holiday by insisting on calling the WTC site "hallowed ground."

The earliest reference to 9/11 hallowedness I uncovered was published in the Sept. 13, 2001, *Oregonian,* where a sportswriter called "Lower Manhattan and the Pentagon" hallowed ground. A story in the Sept. 18, 2001, *Pittsburgh Post-Gazette* about the airliner that went down in Pennsylvania quotes the brother of one of the flight's victims. He called that crash site "hallowed ground" and added, "When you think of it, it was our first victory against the terrorist threat."

Over on the television side, on Sept. 20, 2001, Jane Clayson of CBS's "The Early Show" and Katie Couric of NBC's "Today," both called the WTC site "hallowed ground." Clayson's usage indicated that the idea had already gained currency. "But so many people see that site now really as hallowed ground, because there are thousands of bodies that are entombed there. I mean, should we build a structure on that site?" Clayson said. On NBC, Katie Couric offered, "Given the lives lost, it should be hallowed ground."

Seeing as we don't live in a religious state, all protestations about WTC hallowedness are just loopy poetry and bad metaphor.

What Hallowed Ground Means

Politicians and pundits across the board embraced the hallowed-ground concept, even if they didn't all agree on how that hallowed ground should be treated. [New York politician] Jack Kemp wrote that the WTC site was hallowed the way the Gettysburg battlefield was hallowed. Rudolph Giuliani called it a "hallowed ground" and a "burial ground" but thought part of it should be developed.

Even today, as construction of the new WTC proceeds, politicians still pay lip service to the hallowed ground. Speaking last month about the dispute over the nearby Islamic center, President Barack Obama said, "I understand the emotions that this issue engenders. Ground Zero is, indeed, hallowed ground."

A Religious Concept

Does the hallowedness of the WTC site derive from the fact that so many died there? Or does it derive from the way they died? I say neither. There is no getting around the fact that hallowedness is a religious concept. Something can't become hallowed all by itself—not even a cemetery. It takes a religious rite to render something sacred and holy, and no such consecrating words were spoken over the WTC site. But even if one had been conducted, would it be binding on nonbelievers? I think not. Seeing as we don't live in a religious state, all protestations about WTC hallowedness are just loopy poetry and bad metaphor. The Pentagon, also struck by the 9/11 jihadists, has its memorial, but almost nobody calls that crash site hallowed.

Hallowed Ground as a Weapon

Charles Krauthammer used the hallowed dodge in his *Washington Post* op-ed as a way to argue against the construction of the Islamic center.

"When we speak of Ground Zero as hallowed ground, what we mean is that it belongs to those who suffered and died there—and that such ownership obliges us, the living, to preserve the dignity and memory of the place, never allowing it to be forgotten, trivialized or misappropriated," Krauthammer wrote.

A Profane Site

But if Ground Zero belongs to those who suffered and died there, why is [developer] Larry Silverstein building on it? Because he acquired the site. The place is not sacred.

It's profane. Just look at the property records. All of this talk about hallowed ground is a lame attempt to leverage ownership of 9/11—something that can't be owned, I've already insisted—and to commandeer the collective memory of the attacks. Don't the people who can't stop talking about hallowed ground realize that they're the ones who are needlessly politicizing the slaughter?

I'm all for remembering the murdered, preserving dignity and memory, and even building memorials. I don't defile graveyards. I don't desecrate churches, synagogues, mosques, or Buddhist temples. I don't burn Qurans. I respectfully observe funeral motorcades. I blaspheme, but that's my own business. But I draw the line at spiritualizing the WTC site and its vicinity. We honor the dead not by fetishizing the memory of their gruesome death but by respecting the living.

8

Conservative Opponents of the WTC Mosque Desecrate Ground Zero

Adam Weinstein

Adam Weinstein is the copy editor for Mother Jones *magazine and a staff writer for* Current Intelligence *magazine.*

The Park51 project, also known as the Ground Zero mosque, has come under attack from Americans who target Muslims and Muslim Americans out of fear, intolerance, and in some cases racism. This negativity is being stoked and channeled by neoconservative intellectuals and cynical politicians engaged in their own political machinations. The intolerance of these groups is a betrayal of American ideals as well as the people who died on September 11. America needs to rediscover its essential pluralism and commit itself to the values that make it exceptional.

Every cloud-piercing building in Manhattan is a holy church of one sort or another. Regardless of its function or of the liturgy presented within, each structure has always stood as an advertisement for pluralism, America's One True Religion. This is New York City, won by Dutch explorers from its natives not in battle but in a transaction, while in Europe, caissons and kingly heads still rolled in brutal wars of empire, succession, and faith. This is a city acquired by the English, converted into "American," and then settled by speakers of every tongue on Earth. In such close contact, the émigrés compete, and there are occasional struggles, riots, street crimes. But the competition is just that: a game, rather than a war. A great faith was built upon such games.

Since 1971, one church with its twin spires stood at the center of this faith. From one of its columns—the Top of the World, the observation deck on Floor 107 of the World Trade Center's South Tower—one could view the One True Religion's other great temples: Ellis Island, where some of my ancestors, the Donigers and the Weinsteins, cemented their conversion; Manhattan's Lower East Side, where they lived among the other immigrant poor; the Statue of Liberty, that most supreme of pilgrim shrines.

9/11 Memories

On September 11th, 2001, I had planned a Manhattan pilgrimage of my own. It was Tuesday of the second week in my senior year at Columbia [Univeristy], and I'd intended to wake at a dark hour and ride the No. 1 train down to the first stop in Brooklyn. Once there, repeating a path I'd trod in earlier years, I'd walk the Brooklyn Bridge, pausing in the middle of its boardwalk to face south and take in the sunrise over New York Harbor: to the left, the Verrazano Narrows Bridge and the Atlantic beyond its span; to the right, Lady Liberty. If I'd timed the trip right, they'd be connected—asphalt, ocean, and bronze, an American trinity—by a ribbon of sunshine. It would breach the horizon, then climb 'til its light and its heat reached the spot on the bridge where I was standing. Satisfied that east was still east, and the sun was where it should be— over *this* place I'd descend into Manhattan, to the World Trade Center [WTC], down to the massive bookstore in its sub-level shopping promenade, there to continue my real education.

Things didn't turn out the way I'd planned on that day. I awoke late and alone in a dorm room, the sun already flashing through the window. Stepping into the hall, I noticed a crowd gathering at the hall's far end, leaning out of its south-facing window. I approached, and I saw the smoke.

It was the beginning of a very long day. Against my parents' advice—it had taken an hour to get through on a cell phone—I took a cab to Union Square. From there, I walked to an elderly friend's office to check on her. I wanted to give blood on the way, but there was already a line of NYU [New York University] students and professors snaking four blocks around Beth Israel Medical Center. Upon finding my friend and sharing a good cry, we made our way on foot up Park Avenue to Grand Central Station. Rumor had it trains were still running out of the city from there. Everyone walked. Public transport had come to a standstill, and taxis were price gouging. Yet business owners, doormen, and church elders lined the sidewalk, offering the trekkers free food, drink, and a place to rest. It was the greatest act of collective sincerity and kindness I have ever witnessed.

In that moment when our great temple was lost and so many parishioners were interred in its rubble, when we needed our faith the most, it was shaken.

An Attack on America

It is fashionable to call what happened that day an "attack on America." That's what it was, strictly speaking. As I stood near Broadway and 18th Street that afternoon, watching the towers' ash clouds rise on the harbor wind and blow out to Brooklyn, Chic Burlingame, a retired Navy officer and fighter pilot, passed the final moments of his life herded to the rear of a hijacked American Airlines jet that would strike the outer ring of the Pentagon. He had been the captain of that American Airlines flight. The Pentagon, in a sadly ironic twist, had been Chic's last duty station before his retirement from the Naval Reserve. He was also a friend; he had recruited me into the

Navy, and mentored me during my brief military career. Chic, his passengers, and the Trade Center victims were joined in death by the occupants of a United Airlines flight that, a short while later, smashed into the ground outside Shanksville, Pennsylvania. In cities all across the nation, families and friends experienced very real losses—and in the sudden, bold violence of the act, they wondered what or who else could be lost.

It *was* an "attack on America." And the site where the Twin Towers stood *is* "hallowed ground." And yet. The people today who are likeliest to employ those phrases are also the least likely to appreciate the American faith that the towers and their city embodied. On the lower end of the intellectual spectrum, these critics are the insular drones of militant Americanism, people who think New York's melting-pot mentality is an enabler of evil, rather than a desirable social end. They fail (or refuse) to recognize that Lower Manhattan was hallowed long before 9/11, by the African slaves (at least some of them Muslim) buried in its earth; by the New York Dolls strip club on West Broadway, and the flophouse motels and Buffalo-wing saloons that flank it; by the homeless huddling in the Park Place and WTC subway stations; by the sheer diversity of humanity that had long lived, worked, and died in this place.

Good Intentions Squandered

But those drones have their priests at the high end of the spectrum, neoconservative intellectuals and political tastemakers engaged in their own cynical games of conquest. When the towers fell, those priests and their ministry emerged as if from nowhere. In that moment when our great temple was lost and so many parishioners were interred in its rubble, when we needed our faith the most, it was shaken. We needed to know the significance of it all, the reason for it. We needed to know it would be all right, that justice would be done.

In that moment, we could have redoubled our faith in the America that is New York. We could have affirmed the sentiment offered us by 60,000 solemn Iranians (*Iranians!*) observing a minute of silence in [capital of Iran] Tehran's largest soccer stadium—a sentiment epitomized in *Le Monde*'s September 12 front-page headline: "*Nous sommes tous Américains* ["We are all Americans"]." We could have ushered in a new era of cosmopolitanism, not only abroad, but on United States territory, from Guam to the newly-christened Ground Zero.

We could have. But we didn't. We needed war—for, as journalist Chris Hedges wrote, war is a force that gives us meaning. And it continues to, not just abroad, but at Ground Zero.

War

Of course, *some* war seemed reasonable in 2001. I rejoined the military hoping to serve in Operation Enduring Freedom, the campaign to defeat the Salafist Islamic militants of Al Qaeda and their Afghan state sponsors, the Taliban. I left the service shortly after, the hunt for Al Qaeda bogged down in open-ended occupation and its architects, rather than pressing for a comprehensive Afghan victory, shifted their focus to Iraq. This reflected the neoconservative pathos among the George W. Bush administration and its supporters, something contrary to the cosmopolitan, pluralist faith seen in New York. Intellectuals, civil servants, and journalists—names like Kristol, Cheney, Rumsfeld, Wolfowitz, Krauthammer, Gerecht—led the way. Theirs was an interventionist, exceptionalist US foreign policy that stood in contrast to neoliberalism; simpler, less pluralist, more muscular. In this worldview, "America" was a singular beacon of right, and all who resisted it in any way were monolithically wrong. As a mythos for explaining the American people and their tribulations, it was attractive all the more for its inelegance. As a foreign policy, it was a disaster.

That the neocon tendency could have dominated the past eight years of foreign policy discourse in America is no surprise. It dovetailed nicely with post-9/11 *domestic* discourse in American locales far removed from New York City, places protected by their provinciality and their homogeneity. Inner America. Not just a physical place, but a mental one, too, metastasized to every corner of the nation. It is the id of a state, unrestrained by a superego. Its hallmarks are American exceptionalism, xenophobia, muscular Judeo-Christianity, and the privileging of emotional arguments over intellectual ones. It believes that diversity and dissent—the very broad bases of the nation's civic faith before 9/11—invite national weakness and ruin.

Targeting Islam

To the neocon priests and their flock in Inner America, one group has always been more monolithically wrong than all others: the world's Muslims. It's been said that a conservative is a liberal who has been mugged by reality. Neoconservatives and Inner Americans, then, must be liberals who have been mugged by reality, and blame it on Islam. Before North Korea, before China, neocons and Inner Americans perceived their greatest enemies to be in the Middle East and South Asia, and they prescribed military intervention accordingly. In doing so, they had to perform the most incredible of mental gymnastics, conflating the Salafist Al Qaeda threat with the Shi'ite revolutionary government in Iran and, of course, the nationalist dictatorship of Saddam Hussein in Iraq. In the event, neoconservatism brought us no justice or closure in Afghanistan. It brought us woe in Iraq, it deepened our nation's financial ruin, and it cemented our global reputation as profilers and torturers of minorities. In short, it proved itself a spectacular failure; Barack Obama, a centrist Democrat who advocated a liberal, multilateral foreign policy and an eventual end to America's expeditionary wars, was to be its antidote.

Despite all of that, Inner America is resurgent, and so are its priests. Two years of the Obama presidency have proven insufficient to restore America's prosperity and prestige. In fact, to Inner America, this administration and its supporters represent a further assault on their Manichaean worldview [the basic conflict between pure good and pure evil], an advance of the very diversity and dialogue they believe dilute their "American" values. The president is, after all, a multiracial man with a funny name, tied by his detractors to the Islamic world. He is a deceiver and a usurper to them. His rise to power, rather than ushering in a post-racial era in the United States, has emboldened Inner America to declare openly its antagonism to all that is different, alien, potentially subversive.

The Park51 Project

The current object of this ire is a new structure planned on Park Place, two blocks from where the northernmost of the Twin Towers stood. This is Park51, a Muslim-oriented community center also known as the Cordoba House or the "Ground Zero Mosque." It's a space meant to propagate the same faith the Towers represented: not Islam, but rather, pluralism. In the end, it will be the only sort of sacred space Manhattan really knows, an upward-stretching column of steel and glass, a windbreak and a place of communion for the city's densely packed multitudes.

[The anti-mosque movement] became a national referendum, not merely on how a parcel of private property near Ground Zero was to be developed, but on how Muslims fit into the founding story America tells itself.

Spearheading the Park51 plan is 62-year-old Feisal Abdul Rauf, a Columbia-educated Sufi Muslim who has lived in New York since the 1960s and has led a mosque in the city for 27 years. Rauf is something of a jet-setter, a frequenter of panels at the World Economic Forum and the Aspen Institute. He seems to aspire to de facto leadership in the American Muslim community, becoming a best-selling author and Islamic mega-church patrician in the mold of Christian pastors like Rick Warren and Joel Osteen. By building flocks around child day-care, Starbucks coffee, and arena big-screen TVs, those pastors have fused economic success—the universal standard of American achievement—with soul saving and mainstream acceptance of their convictions. Rauf clearly hopes his Lower Manhattan center, replete with basketball court, auditorium, and yes, a mosque, will earn him the same acclaim. In that way, the Arab-born Muslim could not be more loyal to American values.

That's not the way Inner America sees it. Early last May [2010], in the midst of a contentious national midterm election campaign, a bombastic right-wing blogger named Pamela Geller wrote a blog post titled "Monster Mosque Pushes Ahead in Shadow of World Trade Center Islamic Death and Destruction." In it, she described Park51 as "Islamic domination and expansionism. The location is no accident. Just as Al-Aqsa was built on top of the Temple in Jerusalem." As *Salon* has pointed out Geller has also claimed that Obama is literally the child of former Nation of Islam minister and American dissident Malcolm X. After beating the battle drums for several more months, Inner America's lay clergy began to take note, vice presidential also-ran Sarah Palin, philandering former congressional speaker Newt Gingrich, and ex-New York mayor Rudy Giuliani had all joined a chorus condemning the "Ground Zero Mosque" and demanding that it be located elsewhere.

The Opposition

Ground Zero Mosque opponents include Debra Burlingame, my old friend Chic's sister. When he died, she founded a group called "9/11 Families for a Safe & Strong America," which endorsed the Iraq war and Bush's reelection in 2004. She also joined forces with Liz Cheney, the former vice president's daughter, and neocon William Kristol to form "Keep America Safe," a right-wing lobby group that "believes the United States can only defeat our adversaries and defend our interests from a position of strength." According to Debra, a former New York–based CourtTV producer, Imam Rauf is one such adversary:

> 9/11 was more than a "deeply traumatic event," it was an act of war. Building a 15-story mosque at Ground Zero is a deliberately provocative act that will precipitate more bloodshed in the name of Allah. Those who continue to target and kill American civilians and U.S. troops will see it as a symbol of their historic progress at the site of their most bloody victory. Demolishing a building that was damaged by wreckage from one of the hijacked planes in order to build a mosque and Islamic Center will further energize those who regard it as a ratification of their violent and divinely ordered mission: the spread of shariah law and its subjugation of all free people . . .

Thus born ugly, the anti-mosque movement quickly grew grotesque. It became a national referendum, not merely on how a parcel of private property near Ground Zero was to be developed, but on how Muslims fit into the founding story America tells itself. In California, a mosque-construction plan became a protest target for conservatives. In Florida, a "charismatic" Christian church has chosen to commemorate 9/11 this year by burning Korans. And in Tennessee—where a right-wing candidate for office doubted aloud whether the "cult" of Islam deserved First Amendment protection—a Murfreesboro Muslim center was firebombed in late August [2010], members of its congregation shot at while surveying the damage. In local online news coverage of the shooting, a commenter calling himself "CanYouHearUsNow" left the following message for all to see: "Sorry ragheads, but you're not in new york city here. BOOM ... BANG ... BOOM."

The Myth of Sensitivity

Some of Inner America's wiser priests—that is, the neoconservatives—recognize the tenuousness of directly attacking a religion in a nation founded on religious freedom. And so they've reframed the debate as one that recognizes Rauf's fundamental religious liberty ... but hopes he'll exercise it elsewhere, out of sensitivity to the families of those killed at Ground Zero. Karen Hughes, the Bush administration official once assigned the unenviable task of explaining US foreign policy to the Arab and Islamic worlds, wrote in the *Washington Post* that moving Park51 would be "a powerful example" of sensitivity to Americans who "are neither anti-freedom nor anti-Muslim; they just don't believe it's respectful." This call for sensitivity and respect comes from a conservative faction that's lambasted Obama and his judicial nominees for displaying what the detractors called an excess of "empathy" in jurisprudence.

The neoconservative Reuel Marc Gerecht, advancing an argument made by his fellow neoconservative Charles Krauthammer, furthered the "sensitivity" frame by writing in the *New Republic* that Rauf should be permitted to have his mosque *only* if he passes a litmus test:

> Charles Krauthammer is right: Ground Zero is sacred ground. It would be morally obscene to allow Muslims to build a center near Ground Zero who had not unequivocally denounced (renounced, would be okay, too) the ideas that gave us the maelstrom of 9/11 ... So we need to know whether Mr. Rauf is a moderate Muslim.

It's telling that Gerecht used the words "obscene" and "moderate" in such close proximity; I suspect he defines the latter much the same way Supreme Court Justice Potter Stewart once famously defined the former "I know it when I see it." In fact, Gerecht's chief guidance on the matter of "Who is a moderate?" was thus: "We get to use American definitions for anything that happens on American soil." Apparently he knows an "American" definition when he sees one, too. Would that the other 300 million of us all agreed.

The Banality of Evil

Taken together, Hughes' and Gerecht's cool analyses represent the most banal of evils. We've heard these arguments before. We heard them when America was segregated by race, when blacks were told that they could work and live separately . . . but should know their place and seek not to provoke white society. Most recently, we've heard it in the debate over full civil rights for gays and lesbians, whose "sinful lifestyle" is alleged to threaten the sanctity of marriage . . . in a nation where half of all matrimonial bonds are torn by divorce.

There is another parallel, of course. Just as Gerecht asks Muslims to verify their moderateness (and thus their suitability to Americanness), some of my ancestors were once asked how Jewish they were, and how German they were—for, they were told, they couldn't be both. Just as easily as Hughes asks Muslims to move away from Ground Zero, some of my ancestors were asked, then forced, to separate themselves from acceptable society, to ghettoize, where they could live in *relative* freedom . . . until they couldn't.

To seek to marginalize Muslims is to repudiate not only Islam, but America's own civic faith.

Making Discrimination Fashionable

When anti-Semitism dogged most of my ancestors, they fled for America, the sanest, safest haven that Jews, whom much of the world would not recognize as human, could hope for.

They had been accused of attacking Gentile civilization with many weapons: faith, wealth, socialism. Of course, there were Jewish partisans and terrorists, from stalwart communist intellectuals to the Stern Gang in Palestine. But that was not *Judaism*, and America was wise enough to discern between a faith and its most extreme adherents.

What was so unthinkable at one time in America—systematic, wholesale, mainstream anti-Semitism—has become, by analogy, fashionable. "This is like a metastasized anti-Semitism," Daisy Khan, Rauf's [wife], recently said of their plight. The Muslims of the United States in 2010 are the Jews of Europe in 1910. In each case, a marginal minority is told to stay marginal, and failing to do so is construed as a threat to "mainstream" society.

In America, this argument has always been a canard at best. In America, mainstream society has always existed in constant flux and compromise. It's reflected in the faith of pluralism, the one that sanctified New York and its Twin Towers long before they fell. To seek to marginalize Muslims is to repudiate not only Islam, but America's own civic faith.

A Shameful Debate

Regrettably, neocons and Inner Americans have succeeded in a remarkable reframing of reality. Supporters and attackers of the Park51 site now accuse each other of insensitively rewarding the terrorists who *actually* planned the 9/11 massacre. They debate the "sensitivity" of allowing Muslims to have the same rights that all Americans theoretically enjoy.

It's tempting to join this fray. It's tempting, also, to agree with New York Governor David Paterson that "the longer we have this feud, the more the terrorists are laughing." There's evidence to support his argument. Counterterrorism expert Evan Kohlmann recently told the *New York Times* that commentators on jihadist forums consider the controversy proof "that the U.S. is hypocritical and that most Americans are enemies of Islam," and that the anti-mosque crowd's sentiments "were feeding anti-American sentiment that could provoke violence."

Such arguments, though seductive, concede the anti-Park51 frame, in which the decision to build a mosque becomes a geopolitical issue rather than a free American's matter of conscience. That is precisely what Inner Americans want. It empowers them to blame American faith in diaspora, America's social and cultural openness, for its vulnerability to violent attack. As Debra Burlingame's statement makes clear, Inner Americans seek to supplant American pluralism with Fortress America. To guarantee "homeland security," they would "secure our borders" and put "freedom on the march," to use a favorite Bush line.

But freedom doesn't march. It breaks step.

The Ugly Side of America

That fact will be seen and felt on September 11 this year [2010], I think. The anti-Rauf crowd plans a mass rally against Park51 at Ground Zero. We've had a taste of how that rally will unfold. On August 23, a rabble demonstrated at the site, and this was how they consecrated their hallowed ground: by verbally assaulting a (non-Muslim) Ground Zero worker wearing a skull cap, by touting keffiyeh-clad effigies of Muslim "terrorists" straddling dummy missiles; by carrying signs that read "NO CLUBHOUSE FOR TERRORISTS!", "SHARIA" and "ISLAM=SLAVERY". At least one protester threatened that if Park51 is built, "We will bombard it."

Such pathos seems incapable of appreciating the irony and the suicidal tendency implicit in repeating this circus at Ground Zero on 9/11, with the nation watching and wanting only to remember its loss. The intellectual impoverishment of the political right, neoconservatives, and their Inner America will be on display, boiled down to a simple fact that in order to save their "hallowed ground," they desecrated it with this gross display of know-nothingism.

The Alternative

There is an alternative, of course. It's explained in a post by the essayist and Lower Manhattan native Mira Schor, titled "My Whole Street Is a Mosque":

> Several times a day, small groups of Muslim men, mainly African street vendors who peddle carvings or fake Vuitton bags and Rolex watches on Canal Street, pull out prayer mats, often just rolls of cardboard they store in the nooks and crannies of the buildings around, they take their shoes off in all weather, wash their feet with water from bottles, kneel towards the East and pray, fourteen blocks from Ground Zero, on ground they've spontaneously "hallowed." And the only thing one can say, in the words of my Holocaust refugee Polish Jewish mother, is "Only in America."

Or, at least, only in New York, where these outdoor rituals take place on the street surrounded by crowds of Chinese vendors, NYPD [New York Police Department] cops, business men, rich men's children and their nannies, and busloads of women tourists from the American South. . . . It is an example of the religious freedom and tolerance that makes this country truly great.

Stories like Schor's—stories that all New Yorkers know—give me hope. Not only that Park51 will be built, but that Inner America will give way to a greater America, one that recalls its essential pluralism. At bottom, the Park51 debate isn't about Al Qaeda and the attacks of September 11. It's about preserving the best of America, the freedom to break step with conventions and customs and sensitivities. I will rest as easily as any of my countrymen when Osama Bin Laden, Ayman Al-Zawahiri, and the other architects of 9/11 have been dealt that which they saw fit to impose on so many innocents. But I would rest even easier knowing that the diaspora is safe, that innocence and diversity are not only still possible in America, but that they *are* America.

The Proposed Ground Zero Mosque Offends Americans' Sensibilities

Newt Gingrich

Newt Gingrich is an author, historian, political commentator, and a former congressman and Speaker of the House of Representatives.

Building an Islamic mosque a few blocks away from the site of the September 11, 2001, terrorist attacks, which were perpetrated by radical Islamists bent on destroying a free America, is a provocation and offends most Americans' sensibilities. For radical Muslims, the Ground Zero mosque is a symbol of triumph over American values and a spark that could set off a grand challenge to civilization. Well-meaning Muslims should insist that such a controversial building be moved, out of sensitivity to victims' families.

One of our biggest mistakes in the aftermath of 9/11 was naming our response to the attacks "the war on terror" instead of accurately identifying radical Islamists (and the underlying ideology of radical Islamism) as the target of our campaign. This mistake has led to endless confusion about the nature of the ideological and material threat facing the civilized world and the scale of the response that is appropriate.

Radical Islamism is more than simply a religious belief. It is a comprehensive political, economic, and religious movement that seeks to impose sharia—Islamic law—upon all aspects of global society.

Many Muslims see sharia as simply a reference point for their personal code of conduct. They recognize the distinction between their personal beliefs and the laws that govern all people of all faiths.

The Radical Islamist

For the radical Islamist, however, this distinction does not exist. Radical Islamists see politics and religion as inseparable in a way it is difficult for Americans to understand. Radical Islamists assert sharia's supremacy over the freely legislated laws and values of the countries they live in and see it as their sacred duty to achieve this totalitarian supremacy in practice.

Some radical Islamists use terrorism as a tactic to impose sharia but others use non-violent methods—a cultural, political, and legal jihad [holy war] that seeks the same totalitarian goal even while claiming to repudiate violence. Thus, the term "war on terrorism" is far too narrow a framework in which to think about the war in which we are engaged against the radical Islamists.

Sharia and Western Civilization

Sharia law is used in many Muslim countries to justify shocking acts of barbarity including stoning, the execution of homosexuals, and the subjugation of women. Sharia does not permit freedom of conscience; it prohibits Muslims from renouncing their Islamic faith or converting to another religion. Sharia does not support religious liberty; it treats non-Muslims as inferior and does not accord them the same protections as Muslims. In these and other instances, sharia is explicitly at odds with core American and Western values. It is an explicit repudiation of freedom of conscience and religious liberty as well as the premise that citizens are equal under the law.

Thus, the radical Islamist effort to impose sharia worldwide is a direct threat to all those who believe in the freedoms maintained by our constitutional system.

Creeping Sharia in the United States

In some ways, it speaks of the goodness of America that we have had such difficulty coming to grips with the challenge of radical Islamists. It is our very commitment to religious liberty that makes us uncomfortable with defining our enemies in a way that appears linked with religious belief.

However, America's commitment to religious liberty has given radical Islamists a potent rhetorical weapon in their pursuit of sharia supremacy. In a deliberately dishonest campaign exploiting our belief in religious liberty, radical Islamists are actively engaged in a public relations campaign to try and browbeat and guilt Americans (and other Western countries) to accept the imposition of sharia in certain communities, no matter how deeply sharia law is in conflict with the protections afforded by the civil law and the democratic values undergirding our constitutional system.

Examples of Sharia

The problem of creeping sharia is most visibly on display in France and in the United Kingdom, where there are Muslim enclaves in which the police have surrendered authority and sharia reigns. However, worrisome cases are starting to emerge in the United States that show sharia is coming here. Andy McCarthy's writings, including his new book *The Grand Jihad*, have been invaluable in tracking instances in which the American government and major public institutions have been unwilling to assert the protections of American law and American values over sharia's religious code. Some examples include:

In June 2009, a New Jersey state judge rejected an allegation that a Muslim man who punished his wife with pain for hours and then raped her repeatedly was guilty of criminal sexual assault, citing his religious beliefs as proof that he did not believe he was acting in a criminal matter. "This court believes that he was operating under his belief that it is, as the husband, his desire to have sex when and whether he wanted to, was something that was consistent with his practices and it was something that was not prohibited." Thankfully, this ruling was reversed in an appellate court.

In May 2008, a disabled student at a public college being assisted by a dog was threatened by Muslim members of the student body, who were reluctant to touch the animal by the prescription of sharia. The school, St. Cloud State [University in Minnesota], chose not to engage the Muslim community, but simply gave the student credit without actually fulfilling the class hours so as to avoid conflict.

In a similar instance in November 2009, a high school senior in Owatonna, Minn., was suspended in order to protect him from the threat of violence by radical Islamists when he wrote an essay about the special privileges afforded his Somali Muslim counterparts in the school environment.

In order to accommodate sharia's prohibition of interest payments in financial transactions, the state of Minnesota buys homes from realtors and re-sells them to Muslims at an up-front price. It is simply not the function of government to use tax money to create financial transactions that correspond to a religious code. Moreover, it is a strategy to create a precedent for legal recognition of sharia within U.S. law.

Amazingly, there are strong allegations that the United States now owns the largest provider of sharia financing in the world: AIG.

A One-Way Street

Last month [June 2010], police in Dearborn, Mich., which has a large Muslim population, arrested Christian missionaries for proselytizing at an Arab festival. They were doing so in a legal, peaceful manner that is completely permissible by law, but, of course, forbidden by sharia's rules on proselytizing. Police may say they were trying to prevent an incident, but why should the 1st amendment right to freedom of speech and the exercise of religious freedom be sacrificed in deference to sharia's intolerance against the preaching of religions other than Islam?

Shockingly, sharia honor killings—in which Muslim women are murdered by their husbands, brothers or other male family members for dishonoring their family—are also on the rise in America but do not receive national attention because they are considered "domestic disturbances." (A recent article in *Marie Claire* magazine highlights recent cases and the efforts to bring national attention to this horrifying trend.)

Cases like this will become all the more common as radical Islamists grow more and more aggressive in the United States.

It is in this context that the controversy over the proposed mosque near Ground Zero must be seen.

Exposing Hypocrisy at Ground Zero

There are many reasons to doubt the stated intentions of Imam Feisal Abdul Rauf, the man behind the Ground Zero mosque. After 9/11 he did not hesitate to condemn the United States as an "accessory" to the attacks but more recently refused to condemn [Palestinian militant group] Hamas as a terrorist organization. This is unsurprising considering he has well-established ties to U.S. branches of the [radical] Muslim Brotherhood. He has also refused to reveal the sources of funding for the mosque project, which is projected to cost $100 million.

More importantly, he is an apologist for sharia supremacy. In a recent op-ed, Rauf actually compared sharia law with the Declaration of Independence. This isn't mere dishonesty; it is an Orwellian [as in George Orwell' *1984*] attempt to cause moral confusion about the nature of radical Islamism.

The true intentions of Rauf are also revealed by the name initially proposed for the Ground Zero mosque—"Cordoba House"—which is named for a city in Spain where a conquering Muslim army replaced a church with a mosque. This name is a very direct historical indication that the Ground Zero mosque is all about conquest and thus an assertion of Islamist triumphalism which we should not tolerate.

It is simply grotesque to erect a mosque at the site of the most visible and powerful symbol of the horrible consequences of radical Islamist ideology.

They say they're interfaith, but they didn't propose the building of a mosque, church and synagogue. Instead they proposed a 13-story mosque and community center that will extol the glories of Islamic tolerance for people of other faiths, all while overlooking the site where radical Islamists killed almost 3,000 people in a shocking act of hatred.

A Travesty That Needs to Be Confronted

Building this structure on the edge of the battlefield created by radical Islamists is not a celebration of religious pluralism and mutual tolerance; it is a political statement of shocking arrogance and hypocrisy.

We need to have the moral courage to denounce it. It is simply grotesque to erect a mosque at the site of the most visible and powerful symbol of the horrible consequences of radical Islamist ideology. Well-meaning Muslims, with common human sensitivity to the victims' families, realize they have plenty of other places to gather and worship. But for radical Islamists, the mosque would become an icon of triumph, encouraging them in their challenge to our civilization.

Apologists for radical Islamist hypocrisy are trying to argue that we have to allow the construction of this mosque in order to prove America's commitment to religious liberty. They say this despite the fact that there are already over 100 mosques in New York City.

In fact, they're partially correct—this is a test of our commitment to religious liberty. It is a test to see if we have the resolve to face down an ideology that aims to destroy religious liberty in America, and every other freedom we hold dear.

10

St. Nicholas Church Should Be Rebuilt on the WTC Site

Aaron Goldstein

Aaron Goldstein is a poet and conservative political commentator.

The September 11, 2001, terrorist attack on the World Trade Center (WTC) also destroyed the historic St. Nicholas Greek Orthodox Church, which was established in 1916. There has been a lack of support in rebuilding the landmark, which is shameful in light of the influential support the Ground Zero mosque has received from city and state officials. Rebuilding the church is imperative because it affirms our Judeo-Christian values.

With all the talk of building a mosque in the shadow of the World Trade Center, how many of you knew there was a church that once stood in the shadow of the World Trade Center? And how many of you knew this same church was destroyed on September 11, 2001?

I must confess that until a few weeks ago I wasn't aware that a church was among the property that was leveled in Lower Manhattan that Tuesday morning. When the South Tower collapsed, it took St. Nicholas Greek Orthodox Church with it. All that remained were two religious icons and a handful of liturgical items. Fortunately, no one was inside St. Nicholas at the time of the collapse. But what had been the center of the Greek Orthodox community in New York City for nearly eighty years was wiped out in a matter of seconds.

Inexplicable Inaction

Under the circumstances, one would think a house of worship would be rebuilt forthwith. How many religious institutions in America are destroyed as a result of an act of terrorism? Imagine for a moment that on September 11, 2001, a mosque had been destroyed in the vicinity of the World Trade Center. Don't you think heaven and earth would have been moved to rebuild that mosque? Yet nine years later, not an inch of brick or mortar has been laid down to rebuild St. Nicholas.

As the City of New York was approving plans for the construction of the Ground Zero Mosque, the Port Authority of New York and New Jersey jettisoned a deal that would have permitted the rebuilding of St. Nicholas. Of course, the Ground Zero Mosque has powerful allies with the likes of New York City Mayor Michael Bloomberg and President [Barack] Obama both of whom expressed their support for the mosque as a matter of religious freedom. Yet where were Mayor Bloomberg's tears for St. Nicholas? What does President Obama have to say about the right of the Greek Orthodox community "to build a place of worship and a community center on private property in Lower Manhattan"?

As the City of New York was approving plans for the construction of the Ground Zero Mosque, the Port Authority of New York and New Jersey jettisoned a deal that would have permitted the rebuilding of St. Nicholas.

A Powerful Friend

Despite the obfuscation of Mayor Bloomberg and President Obama, not to mention the obstinacy of the Port Authority, St. Nicholas Greek Orthodox Church is not without friends. None has been more vocal than George Demos, a former prosecutor with the Securities and Exchange Commission, who is currently seeking the Republican nomination for New York's 1st Congressional District. (The GOP [Republican] primary takes place on September 14 [2010] and among his competitors is Christopher Nixon Cox, grandson of the late President Nixon.)

Demos made people sit up and take notice when he issued a statement that read, "Rebuild the Church at Ground Zero, Not a Mosque." He subsequently wrote an open letter to President Obama calling on him to "please stand up and defend our Judeo-Christian values, express your public and unwavering support for St. Nicholas Church, and ensure that it is rebuilt." As of this writing, President Obama has not responded to Demos' letter either privately or publicly. However, Demos has been able to enlist the support of former New York Governor George Pataki as well as Tim Bishop, the incumbent Democratic Congressman who will be Demos' opponent in November if he wins the GOP primary next week. Demos has posted an online petition to gather signatures in support of rebuilding St. Nicholas (to which I have affixed my signature).

Bureaucracy Is to Blame

Earlier this week, Demos took a few minutes away from his busy campaign to speak with me over the phone. Demos, who is Greek Orthodox, reserved most of his displeasure for the Port Authority. He described it as an entity awash in "bureaucratic inertia" and "answerable to no one." He also expressed disappointment with New York Governor David Paterson. Specifically, he took Paterson to task for his appointment of Chris Ward as executive director of the Port Authority. Rebuilding St. Nicholas has not been a priority for Ward, Demos pointed out, and he remains unwilling to meet with church officials.

Regardless of the outcome of the GOP primary, Demos also told me that he would continue to speak out on behalf of St. Nicholas. "This isn't a political issue. This isn't a partisan issue. It is an issue that speaks to our Judeo-Christian values," Demos said. However, he added that if he were to be the nominee and ultimately win election to Congress, he would have "a bigger platform" from which to support the reconstruction of St. Nicholas. [Incumbent Tim Bishop was re-elected—ed.]

11

Journalists Also Suffer from Breathing Dust from the Collapsed Towers

Anthony DePalma

Anthony DePalma is an author, journalist, and writer-in-residence at Seton Hall University in South Orange, New Jersey.

First responders are not the only ones struggling with the health impact of working down at Ground Zero; construction workers, residents, and journalists have also exhibited health effects from the dust clouds that permeated Lower Manhattan after the September 11, 2001, terrorist attack. In particular, journalists have had a hard time, because the government does not consider them to be first responders. Many are in denial about the link between their illnesses and their time down at the World Trade Center site.

Even now, more than seven years later, images of that day remain frightfully raw, in large measure because a legion of photographers and journalists made the unimaginable events of September 11, 2001, all too real. Some happened to be in lower Manhattan when the first plane struck that morning. Some arrived as the first tower collapsed. Others called in favors so they could slip under police barricades or fly over the debris pile while the fires raged. All of them considered themselves lucky to have been able to get so close to the biggest story of their lives.

But their luck also marked them. Being close enough to the tragedy to capture the horror put them close enough to breathe in the dust that exploded with hurricane force from the obliterated towers. Close enough to have the dust work its way into their bodies just as the images of that day worked their way into their minds and hearts.

Several scientific studies have linked the dust—as corrosive as drain cleaner—to a range of medical problems, some chronic and some life-threatening. The tsunami of dust engulfed everyone who was there that day. Some were left with disabilities that curtailed or ended their careers. Some carry physical and emotional scars that they rarely speak about.

What sets journalists apart from the others is that, by and large, they have not been treated like victims, either because of their own denials or because the system does not consider them responders, even though they—like cops and firefighters—rushed toward the doomed buildings as everyone else ran away from them.

At the Scene

Gary Fabiano, a freelance photographer, had been downtown shooting polling booths for what had started out as primary-election day in New York. He was heading back to his agency's office when a call came in on his cell, and he turned right around. He got so close to the towers that when he looked up, he could not see the top of the building coming down at him. But he heard it. "It was like an avalanche of steel and concrete, the steel snapping, the concrete grinding," he says. "It went completely black, then dead silent."

Fabiano and a New York City firefighter tried to outrun the dust cloud. They took shelter in the loading dock of 7 World Trade Center, a building that hours later would also collapse. "There was so much soot and what the fireman told me was pure asbestos in the air we were breathing," he says. "If you took vacuum bags, filled them up with dust and emptied them down your throat, that's pretty much what it felt like."

The 9/11 Dust Clouds

Besides tons of ground-up concrete, the 9/11 dust clouds contained a toxic brew of compounds—including asbestos, lead, benzene, and mercury—that scientists continue to study. What we know so far is that exposure, even for a relatively short time, could burn breathing passages and cause permanent damage. The dust contaminated lungs and could lead to scarring diseases, like fibrosis and sarcoidosis. While the scientific link between dust and disease has not yet been proven with absolute certainty, the dust has been connected to underweight babies born in lower Manhattan, and to a sharp increase in asthma among adults. And the fallout hasn't been limited to physical ailments. A high percentage of individuals caught in the dust cloud developed post-traumatic stress.

Of course, ground-zero journalists are not alone in falling victim to the dust. Hundreds of uniformed responders—police and fire and emergency medical technicians—have left their jobs on permanent disability. Thousands of construction workers who cleared the site, most of the time without the protection of any kind of respirator mask, are suing the city because they got sick. And for thousands who lived, worked, or went to school in the shell-shocked neighborhoods of lower Manhattan, the dust infiltrated nearly every inch of their lives.

In Denial

But what sets journalists apart from the others is that, by and large, they have not been treated like victims, either because of their own denials or because the system does not consider them responders, even though they—like cops and firefighters—rushed toward the doomed buildings as everyone else ran away from them. Some have had to fight with their employers for help, arguing with human-resources officers and compensation lawyers who refused to link illness to dust. Some have simply not told their supervisors they were hurt, fearing that acknowledging an ailment or asking for time off would break a newsroom ethos. "I was astounded to learn that the stigma and shame attached to acknowledging any emotional stress was even greater for journalists than it was for policemen, firefighters, and other emergency responders," says Elana Newman, a psychologist and director of research for the Dart Center for Journalism & Trauma, which addresses the coverage of tragedies and the impact that such coverage has on journalists. Newman and Dart ran a trauma center for ground-zero journalists in 2002. She says that she spent time talking with a broad range of people who survived the disaster, but found that journalists were the least willing to talk about their feelings. Getting them to come to the formal group sessions she organized proved difficult, so she eventually had to conduct meetings in bars and an East Village photography gallery. "Journalists do see themselves as different," she says.

Take Bolivar Arellano, a senior photographer for the *New York Post* who rushed to the World Trade Center [WTC] on the morning of September 11, arriving in time to photograph people falling a thousand feet to their deaths. When the first tower collapsed, Arellano was directly beneath it and shot pictures of it coming down on top of him. He escaped, but was back by the time the second tower collapsed. This time he was blown off his feet and knocked unconscious. When he came to, his right leg was torn open at the knee. "When I got up I must have had ten pounds of dust on my back," Arellano says, during a recent interview on the east side of Manhattan, near where he lives. "I thought, 'I survived the collapse but now I'm going to die by the dust and ash.'"

The Long-Term Effects

Arellano recovered and went back to work. But he wasn't the same. He developed a dry cough that never really went away. He lost his balance, and more. "I also started having emotional problems but I was afraid to say anything to the editors," he says, and that included his son, Juan, the *Post*'s photo editor. In his native Ecuador, Arellano had covered a massacre of students, and he photographed victims in El Salvador during the war there. But 9/11 had scarred his heart as well as his leg. "I couldn't tell anyone that I cried day and night thinking of those people jumping," he says. "They would think that I was an emotionally unstable person."

Arellano eventually received a monetary settlement from the federal government's September 11 Victim Compensation Fund for the injury to his leg. His knee healed, but his breathing problems and emotional stress have never gone away. Four years ago, he retired from journalism. "Last week I was coughing like a dog—that same dry cough as always," Arellano says. "I live with the fear that I'm going to choke and not be able to breathe." He is sixty-four.

Everyone who worked on the rescue and recovery operations at ground zero in 2001 and 2002 was covered by the extended deadline. But not journalists.

A Freelancer's Dilemma

Freelancers have been even more reluctant than staffers like Arellano to admit their troubles to editors and colleagues, certain that turning down an assignment that they are no longer physically capable of doing, or asking for less-stressful assignments, would hurt their careers. "I will never tell them I am sick—never—for the simple reason that I am disposable," says Philippe Gassot, a fifty-two-year-old freelancer who in 2001 was a correspondent for French TV based in Washington,

D.C. On the morning of September 11, he sped up I-95, arriving at ground zero by late afternoon when the air was still opaque with dust and smoke. For the next month, he was at ground zero every day, filming pieces and transmitting them to France.

Gassot flew back to France for Christmas that year, and colleagues there who had seen the huge dust clouds on TV urged him to see a doctor. During the examination, the doctor found that his lung capacity had dropped by 10 percent. Three years later he took a stress test. "The doctor asked me when I had had a heart attack," Gassot says. He thought the doctor was mistaken. "I was always in good health before; I never had any problems, never saw a doctor. Suddenly, I had all kinds of problems, and they put a stent in my vein."

Gassot did stories on the ground-zero workers who signed up for screening and monitoring at the Mount Sinai Medical Center's World Trade Center programs, which are looking after more than 20,000 people who inhaled trade-center dust. But he never enrolled himself because he didn't want to take a chance of someone finding out about his condition.

Journalists Are Excluded

A few years ago, New York State changed its workers' compensation system to help workers who had been injured at ground zero. Typically, a claim must be filed within two years of a work-related injury. But illnesses caused by exposure to contaminants, such as those found in the trade-center dust may not develop until years later. The legislature enacted special provisions to give people who might not be sick now until 2010 to register for the right to file claims far into the future. Everyone who worked on the rescue and recovery operations at ground zero in 2001 and 2002 was covered by the extended deadline. But not journalists.

That bothered David Handschuh, a forty-nine-year-old New York *Daily News* photographer who was caught in the debris from the collapsing south tower. His right leg was shattered, and he developed post-traumatic stress that prevents him from shooting hard news even now. He went to the state workers' compensation board and asked why journalists and photographers were not covered. "They said it was because the legislation does not specifically include members of the media," Handschuh says.

Assessing the Problem

Joseph Cavalcante, a spokesman for the workers' compensation board, says that's true, but that journalists can file the registration form (called a WTC-12) anyway. This way, he says, if the law changes they will be covered. Handschuh acknowledges that getting the legislature to revisit the law and include journalists is a long shot, but he is putting together a case that may end up helping. He has posted a four-page questionnaire on the Web site of the New York Press Photographers Association, asking for specifics about who worked at ground zero, and how doing so has affected them. He has amassed the most comprehensive set of data about photographers and journalists who were injured on 9/11.

So far, 190 media workers have responded. Fifty-seven percent reported having breathing problems after working at ground zero. Nearly 40 percent said they had developed asthma, and half of those who reported having breathing problems said they were still struggling to breathe today. One in three journalists said that the air at ground zero had caused a chronic cough (only 13 percent said they were active smokers and 58 percent said they had never smoked). Nearly 60 percent said they had developed acid reflux, or similar maladies, after 9/11, and most said they still have it. The journalists' problems were not limited to physical ailments. Nearly one in five said they had been diagnosed with post-traumatic stress disorder, and one in four was suffering from depression.

Confronting the Damage

For some, there was no distance at all between the biggest story of their careers and their own lives. On 9/11, Catherine Leuthold, freelance photographer, took the subway into Manhattan and got there in time to photograph both towers collapsing. At one point, she ducked into an abandoned ambulance, grabbed some gauze and wrapped it around her nose and mouth. "I remember thinking it was really bad to breathe this stuff in."

Within days, she started having trouble breathing. A runner, she couldn't even walk briskly for more than a few blocks. Early in 2002, when she was in Hebron to cover the second Intifada, she and a fellow photographer had to run from what sounded like gunfire. She struggled to breathe, and collapsed. Vertigo kept her bedridden for two and a half days. Back in New York months later, she rushed to cover an explosion in Chelsea but ran out of breath so quickly that she knew something had to be wrong. That was followed by another Middle East trip, and the funeral of a Palestinian boy who had been shot by Israeli soldiers. "I was sobbing, and I was taking pictures at the same time, and realizing that I didn't know if I could continue," Leuthold says.

Her breathing problems got worse, the vertigo continued, and Leuthold realized that she had been hurt on 9/11 in ways that she was still figuring out. She felt she needed a drastic change, so in 2006 she left New York for a two-hundred-year-old farmhouse on the Maine coast. She is a landscaper there now, designing gardens and planting bulbs. She teaches photography at a local Montessori school and she still shoots, though nothing resembling hard news.

Survey Results

For many who responded to Handschuh's survey, merely admitting a dust-related ailment raised the fear that it could derail their careers. Thirty percent said that their health problems had affected their careers, and about the same percentage felt that their emotional problems were interfering with their work. And here's the key to understanding ground zero's impact on journalists: nearly half of those who responded (45 percent) said they had been tempted to turn down an assignment that might trigger unwanted emotions. Yet only 25 percent said they had actually refused to take the assignment.

Like most 9/11 health surveys, this one suffers from its reliance on self-reported data. The exception is the New York City fire department, where each firefighter undergoes a yearly physical. That makes it possible to compare pre-9/11 and post-9/11 conditions. The results seem to support some of Handschuh's findings. Fire-department doctors have found, for instance, that many firefighters lost in one year the amount of lung capacity that they might have been expected to lose over the course of a dozen years.

The Case of Keith Silverman

Photographer Keith Silverman is a freelance cameraman with his own video company who worked regularly with *20/20* and other ABC network programs. On September 11, he was preparing to shoot the Fashion Week show at Bryant Park; when the first jet smashed into the north tower, a producer sent him to the trade center. Silverman spent that night and most of the following week videoing firefighters pulling bodies from the trade-center rubble. In all, he worked in the smoke and dust for three months without protective gear. Silverman, who is six-feet tall and weighs 260 pounds, says that it wasn't until 2004 that he first started noticing strange skin rashes on his arms and back. At that time, he was going through a divorce and had lost his health insurance. A friend who is a nurse urged him to see a doctor about the mysterious lumps on his neck and chest. He did, and the tests came back positive for stage 2 Hodgkin's Lymphoma. He was forty-seven at the time. A subsequent CAT scan revealed that he also had pulmonary fibrosis.

Silverman says he didn't expect help from ABC because he was a freelancer, and he was right. It was too late for him to file for workers' compensation in New York. His only option was Social Security disability, but the legal process has been long and grueling. He's been turned down twice, and is appealing his case to a judge. He's also joined the thousands of responders who are suing the city of New York for negligence in the aftermath of 9/11.

Mount Sinai Programs

Silverman could have gotten help from Mount Sinai's monitoring program, but after he signed up for it, he moved to Atlantic City [New Jersey] and never went. At least 113 people who describe themselves as journalists, photographers, or camera operators are among the people enrolled in Mount Sinai's various 9/11 programs. Dr. Philip J. Landrigan, who oversees the programs, says the journalists are "showing pretty much the same problems at roughly the same proportions as anyone else who was down there." Those problems include asthma, sinusitis, interstitial lung diseases, acid reflux, and post-traumatic stress. One of the important findings from Mount Sinai and other studies is that many people who were exposed to the dust in the first few days developed the same complex set of related illnesses. My friend Keith Meyers is one of them. We worked together for more than two decades at *The New York Times*. He is an avid boater who has covered many stories in and around New York's harbor. After 9/11, he used his contacts to talk his way aboard a Coast Guard helicopter that flew over ground zero. He was in the air, with his camera out the open door, as the chopper hovered over the burning debris pile in the days immediately after the collapse. The smoke and gasses from the raging fires mixed with the dust and ash from the collapsed towers in ways that scientists believe made breathing that air at that time particularly hazardous. Meyers wore no protective gear, but he came back with prize-winning photographs.

A Worsening Condition

By 2006, Meyers was barely able to work. He had come down with the whole range of trade-center symptoms—the persistent dry cough, recurring asthma, gastrointestinal reflux disease, and emotional distress. Although he had photographed many grisly events in his career, Meyers was unnerved by the images from 9/11 and the lingering physical impact the dust had on him. He was put on restricted duty, but in time, as his physical problems mounted, even that proved too stressful.

His editors and immediate newsroom supervisors were sympathetic and did what they could to help. But when he put in for workers' comp, he found himself fighting a system set up to handle broken arms, not breathing problems that take years to develop. As I was writing story after story about the environmental and health impact of ground zero, I watched Meyers get sicker and sicker. Because of the articles I was writing, he opened up to me about the hoops he had to jump through as he dealt with corporate medical officers and the Times Company's insurer, who suggested that his asthma was a preexisting condition even though Meyers had regularly passed the Federal Aviation Administration's rigorous Class 1 Flight Physical, which allowed him to fly with and photograph the crew of the space shuttle *Challenger* while they were in training.

News Organizations Must Support Workers

Officials at the *Times* declined to discuss individual personnel issues. But William Schmidt, a deputy managing editor who worked to get help for Meyers, says that dealing with his post-9/11 issues has raised important new considerations for the newsroom. "Whenever we send people into harm's way, we stand behind them and we always will," Schmidt says. "But the kinds of problems and risks that were presented at the WTC site were something new to us and were not as easily understood or assessed."

After years of emotionally draining struggle, Meyers was put on indefinite medical leave. He said he is satisfied with the way the *Times* ultimately resolved his case, and he finally won his workers' compensation case. But winning is a poor way of describing what's happened to him since 9/11. He can no longer shoot photographs or go out on his beloved boat. He declined several requests to discuss his problems on the record, saying it was too painful. But in a brief interview in March 2008 with the *Photo District News*, Meyers, who is now sixty, revealed the sad truth about his situation. "Not working is harder than being sick," he said.

New York State's decision to allow uniformed responders to register for future claims can be seen as a tacit acknowledgement of the bleak future that possibly awaits those who inhaled the dust.

A Wake-Up Call

Bruce Shapiro, the executive director of the Dart Center, called 9/11 "a wake-up call for a lot of news organizations." But with economic gloom hanging over the news industry now, adding the costs of trauma training isn't a priority.

I've spent a lot of time over the last four years interviewing survivors of 9/11, many sick and most full of fear. They told me how the worst thing of all has been dealing with the unending doubt. They feel betrayed whenever insurers or the compensation system or their own bosses question how dust could make anyone sick. Science, medicine, and the courts are searching for certainty before making a definitive link between the dust and disease. But I've learned that absolute certainty can be an elusive goal, and that it has different meanings in the laboratory, in the courtroom, and perhaps in the unspoken ethos of the newsroom.

New York State's decision to allow uniformed responders to register for future claims can be seen as a tacit acknowledgement of the bleak future that possibly awaits those who inhaled the dust. Excluding journalists and photographers from those provisions challenges concepts of fairness and justice. For ground-zero journalists it's painful, but no surprise. "No one wants to say that yes, this existed, because that opens up the door for anyone who was down there to ask for help," says Gary Fabiano, the freelance photographer who took refuge at the loading dock on 9/11. He says he feels helpless to change things for himself, or for others. And he knows that no matter what happened before, the next time there's a catastrophe and the air is poisoned, he'll be expected to rush in, no questions asked.

And he says he probably will.

12

Not Reestablishing Commerce at the WTC Site Is a Blow to Freedom

Steven Malanga

Steven Malanga is a contributing editor for City Journal *and a senior fellow at the Manhattan Institute.*

The terrorist attack on the World Trade Center (WTC) in 2001 was an attack on capitalism and the American way of life. By backing away from reestablishing commerce at the site, politicians and policy makers hand a victory to the enemies of America. Only developer Larry Silverstein, the owner of 7 World Trade Center, was visionary enough to realize that reintroducing trade on the site is a fitting memorial to American values.

The terrorists who attacked the World Trade Center [WTC] on 9-11-01 were striking a blow—a devastating one they hoped—at what they saw as the heart of capitalism and free markets in the United States. But in the aftermath of the attack, what the rest of the world saw was a wounded but game city that quickly pulled itself up off the mat—from the rapid return of the New York Stock Exchange, located just a few blocks from Ground Zero, to the speedy work of putting the city's essential systems back on line and getting companies back to business.

A Parallel Storyline

But even as New York rebounded, a strange, parallel storyline emerged in the planning to rebuild on Ground Zero. Less in-

Steven Malanga, "The Zero at Ground Zero," Manhattan Institute, July 2, 2008. Reproduced by permission.

spiring, the themes of that story were resignation, a lack of faith in free markets, and a perplexing willingness to capitulate to those who would destroy the institutions that are at the heart of our democratic capitalism. There are many players in this parallel storyline, from urban planners who saw the wholesale destruction as an unprecedented opportunity to shape 16 acres of prime city real estate into their version of the 21st century city, which didn't include a return of commerce, to advocacy groups who viewed the site (and the promise of billions of dollars in federal aid) as an opportunity to advance agendas for everything from subsidized housing to a kind of super urban arts community.

Unfortunately, too many political and business leaders lent credibility to this parallel story line. "America's Mayor," Rudy Giuliani [then-mayor of New York], whose own actions had been so heroic on 9-11, seemed so consumed by the grief that, quoting from [Abraham] Lincoln's Gettysburg address, he called for the entire site to become "hallowed ground" free from commerce. His successor, the businessman mayor Michael Bloomberg, displaying a pessimism about the future of the city's economy that was astonishing in an elected official, argued that Lower Manhattan's days as a commercial venue were numbered and the site should be given over to residential building. John Whitehead, the respected former chairman of Goldman Sachs tapped by New York Governor George Pataki to head the rebuilding effort, seemed seduced by the far-fetched schemes of planners and wound up advocating that the site become the center of a tourism district revolving around 9-11—a proposal that smacked of turning Ground Zero into a Disneyland of Death.

All of these voices, and others, have conspired to give us what we have now [in July 2008], which is a site where, approaching seven years after the attack, all one can see for the most part are a bunch of cranes and other machinery moving around dirt. On Monday, the latest report on "progress" at

Ground Zero (and one can only use that word in [quotes] when referring to the WTC site) noted that virtually all of the work there is behind schedule and billions of dollars over budget.

A Mess at Ground Zero

The mismanagement of the site has produced a design for a new transit station that is so expensive and impractical to build that even with a $2 billion budget, it can't be constructed, and probably never will [be]. Meanwhile, the so-called "iconic" Freedom Tower, conceived with no practical commercial purpose in mind so that it will be occupied mostly by government agencies, is a year behind schedule. The construction of the 9-11 memorial dubbed Reflecting Absence—an elaborate but vapid design that commemorates nothing except the absence of those who died that day (with barely even a special nod to the police and fire officers who gave their lives to save others)—is also behind schedule after cost estimates doubled beyond the original $500 million projections. It's now nearly certain that the memorial, reengineered to be on budget, will not open by the 10th anniversary of the attacks [September 11, 2011], while memorials at the Pentagon and in Shanksville, Pa., are already completed. One component of the Ground Zero memorial, an accompanying museum dubbed the International Freedom Center, won't ever open. The redevelopment team shelved it because its content was so controversial.

At this point, the only commerce taking place on the former site of the World Trade Center is in the rebuilt 7 World Trade, which sat to the north of the twin towers and also collapsed that day. Owned by the developer Larry Silverstein, 7 World Trade was never part of the original 16-acre Ground Zero site controlled by the Lower Manhattan Development Corp., and so Silverstein was free to move quickly to rebuild without government intrusion. Shovels hit the ground in May of 2002, and the new, 52-story tower opened in spring of 2006. It boasts more than 1 million square feet of leased space to blue-chip tenants like ABN AMRO, Ameriprise Financial, and Moody's Corp.

Striking a Blow for Commerce

Silverstein should be something of a champion of Ground Zero. Through all of the talk about abandoning commerce at the site and all of the political infighting and pie-in-the-sky planning, he was crucial in fighting to ensure that the 16-acre site didn't simply become parkland, or housing. A year ago he told me, "The financial center's locomotive was the World Trade Center, and for the sustenance of the city and the region, we need to get those jobs back." In addition to 7 World Trade, Silverstein has the right to develop three other towers on Ground Zero, although he's had to wait for the agency controlling redevelopment to design a site plan and do the foundation work for the towers.

For his efforts, Silverstein hasn't been celebrated, but demonized. The Vice Chairman of the Port Authority of New York and New Jersey, which controls the site, called him "greedy" for his tough negotiations with potential tenants of 7 World Trade, which dragged out the announcement of some leases. Mayor Bloomberg accused him of asking too much to lease up 7 World Trade—as if our politicians should be setting office leasing rates. One of the city's tabloids, the *Daily News,* responded to Silverstein's defense of himself with the headline "Butt Out, Larry."

Yet in the end, Silverstein has given us the only real progress at Ground Zero. And he's constructing the real memorial down there, the return of the marketplace on the site where the terrorists eradicated it. To achieve that, it isn't Silverstein or the free market that should be butting out.

Organizations to Contact

The editors have compiled the following list of organizations concerned with the issues debated in this book. The descriptions are derived from materials provided by the organizations. All have publications or information available for interested readers. The list was compiled on the date of publication of the present volume; names, addresses, phone and fax numbers, and e-mail and Internet addresses may change. Be aware that many organizations take several weeks or longer to respond to inquiries, so allow as much time as possible.

Alliance for Downtown New York
120 Broadway, Suite 3340, New York, NY   10271
(212) 556-6700 • fax: (212) 556-6707
e-mail: contactus@downtownny.com
website: www.downtownny.org

The Alliance for Downtown New York, also known as the Downtown Alliance, is a membership organization that promotes Lower Manhattan and advocates for policies to improve the region's economy and quality of life. The Downtown Alliance manages the Downtown-Lower Manhattan Business Improvement District (BID), which provides essential services such as supplemental security and sanitation, streetscaping, marketing and tourist information, and special-events planning. It has been a valuable resource for businesses in the area dealing with the World Trade Center rebuilding process. The Downtown Alliance publishes two e-newsletters, the *Download* and *Destination Downtown*, and offers links to a range of research and other information on Lower Manhattan real estate, retail, business, and residents.

Association for a Better New York (ABNY)
355 Lexington Ave., 8th Floor, New York, NY   10017

(212) 370-5800 • fax: (212) 661-5877
website: www.abny.org

The Association for a Better New York is a nonprofit organization that supports the growth and improvement of New York City. ABNY's coalition of policy makers and political and business leaders contribute innovative ideas to solve the city's challenges, network to find support for those ideas, and then find ways to implement them. Networking is a major component of the organization, which provides a forum for city leaders and activists to come together and exchange ideas in a supportive and constructive way. One of ABNY's central concerns has been the redevelopment of Lower Manhattan, particularly the World Trade Center site.

Families of September 11
1560 Broadway, Suite 711, New York, NY   10036
(212) 575-1878
e-mail: info@familiesofseptember11.org
website: www.familiesofseptember11.org

Families of September 11 is a nonprofit organization established by the families of the victims of the terrorist attacks on September 11, 2001. The group outlines its goals as: providing updated information on relevant issues and articles; advocating to raise awareness about the effects of terrorism and public trauma; and championing "domestic and international policies that respond to the threat of terrorism, including support for the 9/11 Commission Recommendations, and to reach out to victims of terror worldwide." The organization publishes a quarterly e-newsletter as well as action alert e-mails, which can be accessed through the organization's website.

Lower Manhattan Construction Command Center (LMCCC)
One Liberty Plaza, 20th Floor, New York, NY   10006
(212) 442-4500 • fax: (212) 442-4999
website: www.lowermanhattan.info

The Lower Manhattan Construction Command Center is a state-city agency that is responsible for providing the most recent, comprehensive, and user-friendly information about the rebuilding and revitalization of Lower Manhattan. The LM-CCC website links to a virtual tour of the area, offers a video clip chronicling the evolution of Lower Manhattan, and has access to a range of news, speeches, testimony, presentations, and information. Traffic updates and construction alerts are also available for local residents.

Lower Manhattan Development Corporation (LMDC)
One Liberty Plaza, 20th Floor, New York, NY   10006
(212) 962-2300 • fax: (212) 962-2431
website: www.renewnyc.com

The Lower Manhattan Development Corporation is a state-city agency playing a vital role in the planning and coordination of the rebuilding of Lower Manhattan, including the World Trade Center site. Established after the terrorist attacks of September 11, 2001, the agency works with the private and public sectors to shape the future of Lower Manhattan and cement its position as a vibrant and productive sector of the city. LMDC also conducts public hearings, participates in community board meetings, and solicits the feedback of 9/11 families, community and business leaders, civic groups, and policy makers to formulate plans and policies. The LMDC website features the plans for the World Trade Center site, including the memorial and museum; an events listing; an archive of articles; a photo gallery; speeches from officials and civic leaders; and information on key programs.

**National September 11 Memorial and Museum
at the World Trade Center Foundation**
One Liberty Plaza, 20th Floor, New York, NY   10006
(212) 312-8800 • fax: (212) 227-7931
e-mail: info@911memorial.org
website: www.911memorial.org

The National September 11 Memorial and Museum at the World Trade Center Foundation was established in 2005 to work with the Lower Manhattan Development Corporation to design and develop a plan for the September 11 Memorial and Museum. Later, it partnered with the Port Authority of New York and New Jersey to oversee the construction of the project. The group's website offers information on both the memorial and museum, as well as teaching material, an interactive timeline, video, photos, webcasts, and tourist information. The website also features its *Memo Blog*, which provides news and discussion about the National September 11 Memorial and Museum.

New York City Department of Environmental Protection (NYCDEP)
59-17 Junction Blvd., 13th Floor, Flushing, NY   11373
(212) 639-9675
website: www.nyc.gov

The New York City Department of Environmental Protection is the city agency that is responsible for New York City's environment. It manages, protects, and conserves the city's water supply; regulates air quality; monitors the handling and storage of hazardous waste; and deals with the issue of noise pollution. It is also the agency that tested the air quality at the World Trade Center site after the fall of the Twin Towers. The NYCDEP publishes the *Weekly Pipeline*, a weekly newsletter that covers recent news, events, programs, and initiatives, available on the department's website. Speeches, testimony, articles, and press releases can also be found on the agency's website.

Office of the Public Advocate for the City of New York
1 Centre St., 15th Floor, New York, NY   10007
(212) 669-7200 • fax: (212) 669-4701
website: pubadvocate.nyc.gov

The Office of the Public Advocate for the City of New York is a government position tasked with overseeing government agencies and programs and acting as a watchdog on city government on behalf of the people of New York City. The public advocate presides over New York City Council Meetings and can propose legislation. The main activities of the public advocate are consumer protection, government transparency and reform, safety and civil rights, responsible development, fair public budgets, and inclusive public education. Citizens can lodge complaints on the public advocate's website, which also features recent news, press releases, speeches, correspondence with city agencies, videos, photos, and an events calendar.

Port Authority of New York and New Jersey (PANYNJ)

One Madison Ave., 5th Floor, New York, NY   10010
(800) 221-9903
website: www.panynj.gov

The Port Authority of New York and New Jersey is a two-state port district that runs most of the critical regional transportation infrastructure within the port areas of New York and New Jersey, including the bridges, airports, tunnels, and seaports. It also oversees the World Trade Center and is the owner of the World Trade Center site. As such, the port authority works with the developer and the Lower Manhattan Development Corporation on the rebuilding of the World Trade Center. The port authority also offers a monthly e-newsletter, *Growing the Region*, as well as studies and reports on the facilities it manages and ongoing projects. One of the PANYNJ's recent studies is *The Economic Impact of World Trade Center Development*.

September 11th Families' Association

22 Cortlandt St., Suite 801, New York, NY   10007
website: www.911families.org

The September 11th Families' Association is a group of 9/11 family members that "supports victims of terrorism through communication, representation, and peer support." The association strives to unite the September 11th community, advocates for issues important to September 11th families, and finds and shares resources for long-term recovery from the 2001 attacks. They have also had a strong and influential voice in the planning of the World Trade Center Memorial and related legislation. The association's website links to its newsletter, *The September 11th Families Association Tribute*, which offers updates on recent events, initiatives, legislation, and issues of interest to September 11th families.

Bibliography

Books

Allison Blais and Lynn Rasic
A Place of Remembrance: Official Book of the 9/11 Memorial and Museum. Washington, DC: National Geographic, 2011.

Anthony DePalma
City of Dust: Illness, Arrogance, and 9/11. Upper Saddle River, NJ: FT Press, 2011.

Paul Goldberger
Up from Zero: Politics, Architecture, and the Rebuilding of New York. New York: Random House, 2004.

William Keegan Jr. and Bart Davis
Closure: The Untold Story of the Ground Zero Recovery Mission. New York: Simon & Schuster, 2006.

Daniel Libeskind and Paul Goldberger
Counterpoint. New York: Monacelli Press, 2008.

Paul J. Lioy
Dust: The Inside Story of Its Role in the September 11th Aftermath. Lanham, MD: Rowman & Littlefield, 2010.

John Mollenkopf, ed.
Contentious City: The Politics of Recovery in New York City. New York: Russell Sage, 2005.

Philip Nobel — *Sixteen Acres: Architecture and the Outrageous Struggle for the Future of Ground Zero*. New York: Metropolitan Books, 2005.

David Simpson — *9/11: The Culture of Commemoration*. Chicago: University of Chicago Press, 2006.

Deyan Sudjic — *The Edifice Complex: How the Rich and Powerful Shape the World*. New York: Penguin, 2005.

Krzysztof Wodiczko — *City of Refuge: A 9/11 Memorial*. London: Black Dog, 2009.

Periodicals and Internet Sources

Shawn Boburg — "Memorial Museum at Ground Zero Will Not Focus on Bin Laden," *Bergen County (NJ) Record*, May 23, 2011.

Elliot Brown — "New WTC Towers Rise Amid Doubts," *Wall Street Journal*, May 3, 2011.

Linda P. Campbell — "At Ground Zero, Moving on but Never Forgetting 9/11," *Kansas City (MO) Star*, May 17, 2011.

Craig Causer — "WTC Memorial Scheduled to Open in 2009: Stakeholders and Families Continue to Clash," *Non-Profit Times*, September 1, 2006.

Commonweal — "Groundless," September 10, 2010.

Kathleen Foster — "Rise of Freedom: Ground Zero from the Ground Up," Fox News, May 19, 2011. www.foxnews.com.

Free Press (Winnipeg, Canada) — "Squabbles, Politics Infect 9/11 Memorials," September 12, 2007.

Conor Friedersdorf — "If You Build It, Nothing Bad Will Happen," *Forbes*, July 22, 2010. www.forbes.com.

Paul Goldberger — "Test Drive," *New Yorker*, October 12, 2009.

Mehdi Hasan — "Fear and Loathing in Manhattan," *New Statesman*, November 1, 2010.

C.J. Hughes — "A Tale of Two Rebuilding Efforts at Ground Zero," *Architectural Record*, September 2009.

Brian Kates — "No-Work and All Pay at Ground Zero as Rebuilding Costs Up $96 Million Under Lax Union Rules," *New York Daily News*, May 8, 2011.

Robert Kolker — "Inside the Future 9/11 Reliquary," *New York*, September 13, 2010.

Roland Li — "World Trade Center Site Is a Hub of Activity—at Last," *Real Estate Weekly*, November 24, 2010.

Sam Lubell — "At Ground Zero, Little Progress After Seven Years," *Architectural Record*, September 2008.

Peter Maass   "Sanctifying by Attacking," *New York*,
                     August 23, 2010.

Lisa Miller   "War over Ground Zero," *Newsweek*,
                     August 16, 2010.

Lisa Miller   "Feisal Abdul Rauf," *Newsweek*,
                     January 3, 2011.

Tim Moran   "Supplying WTC Site a Major
                     Logistical Challenge," *Real Estate
                     Weekly*, September 6, 2006.

Katha Pollitt   "Ground Zero for Free Speech,"
                     Nation, August 30, 2010.

David Remnick   "Exit Bin Laden," *New Yorker*, May
                     16, 2011.

John Riley   "Ground Zero Construction Making
                     Progress," *Newsday*, May 5, 2011.

Jeff Van Dam   "WTC Cheat Sheet: Construction Is
                     Under Way at Ground Zero—but
                     Not Much of It," *New York*, May 25,
                     2009.

Jim Wallis   "A Test of Character," *Sojourners*,
                     December 2010.

Fareed Zakaria   "The Real Ground Zero," *Newsweek*,
                     August 16, 2010.

Index